AS/A-LEVEL YEAR 1

STUDENT GUIDE

EDEXCEL

Psychology

Social psychology and cognitive psychology (with issues and debates)

Christine Brain

PHIL
HC
ED
AN F

D0412930

Philip Allan, an imprint of Hodder Education, an Hachette UK company, Blenheim Court, George Street, Banbury, Oxfordshire OX16 5BH

Orders

Bookpoint Ltd, 130 Milton Park, Abingdon, Oxfordshire OX14 4SB

tel: 01235 827827

fax: 01235 400401

e-mail: education@bookpoint.co.uk

Lines are open 9.00 a.m.–5.00 p.m., Monday to Saturday, with a 24-hour message answering service. You can also order through the Hodder Education website: www.hoddereducation.co.uk

ISBN 978-1-4718-4342-6

First printed 2015

Impression number 5 4 3 2

Year 2019 2018 2017 2016

This Guide has been written specifically to support students preparing for the Edexcel AS and A-level Psychology examinations. The content has been neither approved nor endorsed by Edexcel and remains the sole responsibility of the author.

Typeset by Integra Software Services Pvt. Ltd., Pondicherry, India

Cover photo: agsandrew/Fotolia

Printed in Dubai

Hachette UK's policy is to use papers that are natural, renewable and recyclable products and made from wood grown in sustainable forests. The logging and manufacturing processes are expected to conform to the environmental regulations of the country of origin.

Contents

Content Guidance

Questions & Answers

■ Getting the most from this book

Exam tips

Advice on key points in the text to help you learn and recall content, avoid pitfalls, and polish your exam technique in order to boost your grade.

Knowledge check

Rapid-fire questions throughout the Content Guidance section to check your understanding.

Knowledge check answers

1 Turn to the back of the book for the Knowledge check answers.

Summaries

■ Each core topic is rounded off by a bullet-list summary for quick-check reference of what you need to know.

Exam-style questions

Commentary on the questions

Tips on what you need to do to gain full marks, indicated by the icon **e**

Sample student answers

Practise the questions, then look at the student answers that follow.

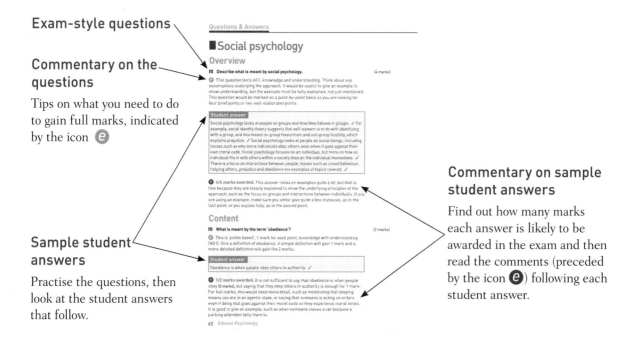

Commentary on sample student answers

Find out how many marks each answer is likely to be awarded in the exam and then read the comments (preceded by the icon **e**) following each student answer.

■ About this book

This guide covers the first two topic areas of the Edexcel AS and A-level Psychology specifications: Topic 1 Social psychology and Topic 2 Cognitive psychology, which are examined in AS Paper 1 and A-level Papers 1 and 3. It also covers issues and debates for the two topics, which are examined on A-level Papers 1 and 3.

Table 1 shows how these three papers fit in the overall AS and A-level qualifications. Note that AS Paper 1 only covers these two topics, while A-level Paper 1 examines these two topics with the addition of issues and debates, plus biological psychology and learning theories. A-level Paper 3 focuses on psychological skills, including the method, studies and issues and debates from social and cognitive psychology.

AS	A-level year 1	A-level year 2
Paper 1: **social, cognitive**	Paper 1: **social, cognitive**, biological, learning (including issues and debates)	Paper 2: clinical and one from criminological, child and health (including issues and debates)
Paper 2: biological, learning	Paper 3: **psychological skills** (method, studies, issues and debates)	

Table 1 Overview of AS and A-level papers (**bold** indicates topics covered in this guide)

Aims

This guide is not a textbook — there is no substitute for reading the required material and taking notes. Nor does it tell you the actual questions on your paper. The aim of this guide is to provide you with a clear understanding of the requirements of AS Paper 1 and A-level Papers 1 and Paper 3, and to advise you on how best to meet these requirements. This guide looks at:

- the psychology you need to know about
- what you need to be able to do and what skills you need
- how you could go about learning the necessary material
- what is being examined, including mathematical skills
- what you should expect in the examination
- how you could tackle the different styles of exam question
- the format of the exam, including what questions might look like
- how questions might be marked, including examples of answers, with exam advice

How to use this guide

A good way of using this guide is to read it through in the order in which it is presented. Alternatively, you can consider each topic in the Content Guidance section, and then turn to a relevant question in the Questions & Answers section. Whichever way you use the guide, try some of the questions yourself to test your learning.

Note that cross-references in the Content Guidance are given to answers in the Questions & Answers section that provide more information on particular areas of content.

Glossary

A list of terms is included at the end of this guide (pages 84–90). They are organised alphabetically and subdivided into the two topic areas — social psychology and cognitive psychology. This is a list of definitions that can help you in your revision. You could also go through the glossary matching terms to topic areas, which will help your learning, picking out all the methodology terms to draw them together.

Content Guidance

■ Social psychology

This section looks at social psychology with its five main parts (content; method; studies; key question; practical investigation). It also has an issues and debates section. In some places in your course you can choose what you study. In this section suitable material is presented, but you may have studied different examples (this is indicated). *You might be better advised to revise the material you chose for your course.*

Table 1 Summary of social psychology in your course

Content
Obedience is examined, with agency theory — which is a way of understanding obedience —as well as social impact theory. Milgram's (a main figure in the field of obedience) main study and three variations are outlined. Factors affecting obedience —personality, gender, situation and culture — are considered. The social identity theory and realistic conflict theory of prejudice are explained and factors affecting prejudice and discrimination too — personality, situation and culture. Individual differences and developmental issues in social psychology covered in your course need to be considered. This is not additional material but is about making links as appropriate.
Methodology
Questionnaires and interviews as research methods are outlined, together with evaluation. Qualitative and quantitative data are outlined as well, again with evaluation, and how analysis is done for both quantitative and qualitative data but not using inferential statistical tests. Four sampling techniques are covered, as are ethical issues in 'doing' psychology, including risk management.
Two studies in detail
Sherif et al. (1954/1961) and Burger (2009) are described and evaluated. You may have studied Reicher and Haslam (2006) or Cohrs et al. (2012) instead.
Key question
The question of how knowledge of social psychology can be used to reduce prejudice in situations such as crowd behaviour or rioting is covered, but you may have looked at one or more different key questions.
Practical
You will have carried out at least one practical within social psychology and you should use your own practical, because you will have 'learned by doing'. Some ideas about the practical are suggested in this book.
Issues and debates*
Unless you are studying at AS, there are 11 issues and debates in your course: ethics; practical issues in the design and implementation of research; reductionism; comparisons of ways of explaining behaviour using different themes; psychology as a science; culture and gender; nature-nurture; understanding of how psychological understanding has developed over time; issues of social control; the use of psychological knowledge in society; and issues related to socially sensitive research. **Issues and debates are not required at AS, but they can be useful for evaluation purposes.*

Social psychology Overview Q1 describes what is meant by social psychology. What follows is a brief summary.

The social approach is about people, both as individuals and as part of a group or groups, and how people live together comfortably — and when they do not.

Content: obedience

Milgram's research into obedience led to him putting forward the agency theory of obedience. Social impact theory is not really a theory of obedience but links well to the study of obedience. Agency theory and social impact theory are outlined in this section, after Milgram's main study is explained with three of his variations.

Obedience means to obey a direct order from an authority figure, even when obeying means going against one's own moral code: an example is a soldier obeying orders.

A main name in the study of obedience is Milgram. You need to know his basic study and three variations of that study.

Social psychology Content Q1 looks at what is meant by the term obedience.

Milgram's 1963 basic study

Milgram aimed to test the idea that 'Germans were different' when they carried out orders to persecute Jews and others during the Second World War. He asked how far 'ordinary people' would go if ordered to administer what they thought were electric shocks to someone else. Use your textbook or some other source to revise the procedure of his study.

Issue	Comment
The participants were volunteers	This made the sample biased — look at strengths and weaknesses of volunteer samples as outlined in the method section (see page 27)
The participants were deceived	They were told it was a study of memory but it was about obedience. They were told that the accomplice was another participant and that the 'shocks' were real — both not true
The participants were not given the right to withdraw fully	They could stop but there were four prods first, which is not in accordance with current guidelines
The experimenter was in the room	They may have felt obliged to continue just because the experimenter was present — and supposedly making sure no harm was done to the 'accomplice'
The study was at Yale University	This is a well-known university with a lot of prestige. The participants would expect things to be under control

Table 2 Some main issues in the procedure

Knowledge check 1

Define social psychology, including two examples.

Exam tip

In the examination, 'definition' questions can be asked, usually for 2 or 3 marks. You get 1 mark for a basic definition, 2 marks if you explain in some detail, and for a third mark it is a good idea to add an example that illustrates the term or concept clearly.

Exam tip

Terms like 'obedience' are not always defined in great detail in the Content Guidance section. Use the glossary as a revision guide and add detail from there to inform your preparation for 'definition' questions. You could use index cards to put a term on one side and a definition with an example on the other and aim for a 3-mark question.

Results

Participants protested — but there was a script, and each time they protested the experimenter followed this script. All of them (100%) went up to 300 volts and 26 of the 40 men (65%) carried on to the end, which was 450 volts. During the study, many participants were very distressed and one even had what was called a full-blown seizure.

Conclusions

Milgram concluded that an ordinary person would obey orders from an authority to an extreme extent even when they were very uncomfortable about doing so.

Strengths	Weaknesses
Good controls avoid bias and mean that the situation was the same for all, so cause-and-effect conclusions could be drawn	The study is unethical because the participants were deceived, did not give informed consent, were distressed and did not have the full right to withdraw
The well-controlled procedures mean that the study is replicable and can be tested for reliability	The study can be said to lack validity because of the artificial procedures (though punishment can be in an artificial situation like a laboratory)

Table 3 Strengths and weaknesses of the basic study by Milgram (1963)

Three variations of Milgram's 1963 study

You need to know three of the variations of the main study: Experiments 7, 10 and 13. There were 19 in all.

Experiment 7: experimenter absent

In Experiment 7 the experimenter is out of sight and giving orders over the telephone. Instead of 26 obeying the orders, 9 obeyed, which is 22.5% compared with 65% — a considerable difference. The conclusion is that if someone wants to be obeyed, they are better off being face-to-face than giving orders over the phone or from a distance.

You can use the evaluation of Milgram's main study as the aims and procedure largely remained the same. More specific evaluation points are included in Table 4.

Strengths	Weaknesses
Comparisons with Milgram's main study and other variations are more fair as he used the same procedure throughout except for the one thing varied	There is a query over the validity of the results (how far they represent real life) if the participant seemed to be wanting to help the experimenter
When in other variations the physical presence of the experimenter was different, it was also found then that that presence did affect the level of obedience	Perhaps the participant trusted the experimenter at such a well-known university not to give others 'real shocks', which of course was well-placed trust

Table 4 Strengths and weaknesses of Milgram's variation, Experiment 7

Experiment 10: institutional context

Milgram wondered whether the well-known setting of Yale University affected the results of his main study, so he set the study up in a run-down office block. Milgram found 47.5% went up to the maximum voltage compared with 65% in the basic study. It was thought that there were factors at work over and above the university setting when it came to obeying orders of an authority figure, even if the setting had some impact.

Exam tip

Considering issues when learning a study will help you both to understand and evaluate the study. Drawing up a table like this one here for studies you are learning will give you good notes to revise from.

Exam tip

When learning the results of a study be sure to learn actual numbers where possible, such as the percentages of participants going to 300 volts and to 450 volts in Milgram's study.

Exam tip

When learning studies and preparing to answer questions about them, it is a good idea to prepare enough for 3 or 4 marks for the aim, and around 6 to 8 marks each for the procedure, results, conclusions, strengths and weaknesses for each study. Remember a 'mark' means giving a point clearly and in some detail.

Content Guidance

Specific evaluation points are included in Table 5.

Strengths	Weaknesses
Using the office block adds to the validity, being a real-world setting, perhaps more real than an experiment in a university	The 'laboratory' feel to the study remained and so possibly the desire to help in building scientific knowledge remained, even though the setting changed
As with the other variations, with procedures kept the same except for the one variation in IV, comparisons can be made between results	19 obeyed (47.5%) to the end compared with 26 so the difference is small. Milgram thought the difference not that great, but others might think it is enough of a difference to say that setting affects obedience

Table 5 Strengths and weaknesses of Milgram's variation, Experiment 10

Experiment 13: ordinary man gives orders

Milgram set up a variation of his experiment where an 'ordinary man' gives the orders. When the experimenter leaves the room, another person who was in the room takes over — in charge but without the grey coat. The other person suggests going up one switch at a time and so is the one giving the orders. In this variation, 4 of the participants, 20%, went to the maximum shock level (16 out of the 20 participants did not). It seems to be the trappings of authority such as a uniform (the grey coat) or the role of the person giving orders (the experimenter) that lead to the high obedience.

Knowledge check 2

Give the results from the three variations you need to know about and explain what conclusion can be drawn in each case.

Specific evaluation points are included in Table 6.

Strengths	Weaknesses
As with the other variations, with procedures kept the same except for the one variation in IV, comparisons can be made between results	There was still a lot of 'authority' in the situation, including the generator, the university setting and backing of Yale University. The findings looked at the actual experimenter but not at all the authority in the study
The 'ordinary man' was seen by the participant as another participant, which would have helped to reduce his/her authority when he/she 'took over' the experiment, and added to validity	Validity can be questioned. Perhaps removing the authority figure made the study even less likely and so the participants did not go along with it for that reason

Table 6 Strengths and weaknesses of Milgram's variation, Experiment 13

Some other variations and their results: for use in evaluation and discussion

Situation/procedures	Result
Original study	26 out of 40 (65%) continued to the end
Two experimenters: at 110 volts, one tells the participant to stop and the other tells the participant to continue (Experiment 15)	All participants stopped
Three teachers (two were confederates): one confederate-teacher stops at 150 volts and the other at 210 volts (Experiment 17)	Only 10% of participants continued to the end
Experimenter's instructions are given by tape and the participant can speak to the experimenter (who is not in the room) by phone (Experiment 7)	9 of the 40 (22.5%) participants continued to the end
Moving the victim closer until the participant held the victim's hand down to receive the shock (Experiment 4)	12 of the 40 participants obeyed (30%)
Held in Research Associates of Bridgeport offices, in a fairly rundown office building (Experiment 10)	19 of the 40 participants obeyed (47.5%)
When the participants were women (Experiment 8)	26 of the 40 obeyed (65%)
Participant chooses the shock level (Experiment 11)	1 obeyed (2.5%)

Table 7 Milgram's variations on his basic study

Ethical issues arising from obedience studies: for use in evaluation and discussion

- Milgram's participants gave consent to a study about learning, but not to a study about obedience and not to give what they thought were strong electric shocks to someone else.
- There was deceit, for example, participants thought the study was about learning, whereas it was about obedience.
- Milgram used verbal prods to keep the participants obeying. The right to withdraw was not given.
- Milgram was competent and he asked the opinion of colleagues about the study.
- Milgram debriefed fully, introducing participants to their 'victim', to show all was well.
- The participants were paid. This is unethical as it means there is a contract, which the participants may not feel able to break.
- There was initially confidentiality — the names of the participants were not published.
- The participants were volunteers recruited through a newspaper advertisement — they chose to take part.
- If a participant became distressed, as one did, observers stepped in to stop the study.
- Milgram consulted other people and it was not thought that they would find such a high level of obedience, so he did not intend the study to be as stressful for the participants.
- Ethical guidelines were not as strong in 1963 as they are today, so it is hard to judge the studies by current ethical guidelines.
- Perhaps a study should be carried out if findings can be useful in making society 'better' for people.

Agency theory

You need to learn two theories that can help to explain obedience, one of which is agency theory.

Questions & Answers

Social psychology Content Q2 explains this theory. What follows is a brief summary.

- People obey because of being in an **agentic state**.
- **Moral strain** is the pressure of doing something against one's feelings of right and wrong.
- When acting as an individual, a person is in an **autonomous state**.
- Gupta (1983) found evidence for the shift of responsibility to the experimenter, suggesting people obey because of being agents of the authority figure. She found obedient males in her study accepted 27.6% of the responsibility; those who did not obey accepted 49.4% of the responsibility.

Exam tip

Explain each ethical point you make fully. For example, saying that a study involved deceit is not enough: you need to show *how* deceit was present in each case. It is also useful to prepare more material than you think might be asked as you are not likely to remember everything you revise.

Exam tip

When giving strengths or weaknesses in an answer, explain your points fully. For example, writing, 'The theory is more description than explanation' is not enough. Saying, 'It does not add much as explanation of obedience to say that people obey because they are agents of authority if that is the definition of obedience' is better.

Strengths	Weaknesses
The findings of the variations on Milgram's study back up the theory, because the less they were agents (for example, when the experimenter was not in the room), the less they obeyed	Social power theory is an alternative explanation. In Milgram's studies, the experimenter had reward power, legitimate power and expert power, so could have been obeyed because of being powerful
The theory helps to explain real-life situations such as the Holocaust, where obedience was well beyond what would be expected of autonomous human beings	The theory is more a description than an explanation. Obedience is defined as obeying an authority figure, so saying that people obey because they are agents of an authority figure does not add much

Table 8 Strengths and weaknesses of agency theory as an explanation for obedience

Social impact theory

The other theory you need to know is social impact theory — the way people act in the presence of others, including being obedient. Social impact theory looks at how the opinions of others (individuals and groups) affect us. Latané and Wolf (1981) suggested that groups affect an individual's attitudes depending on the size and status of the group. Milgram found that when someone else disobeyed, a participant was also more likely to disobey, which suggests that behaviour is affected by the presence of others (Experiment 17).

The impact of others on someone's attitudes depends on:

- the number of other people in the environment
- the immediacy of the impact (such as whether the message is given by people you know)
- the strength of the impact (such as the persuasion power of those giving the message)

This means that if more people are giving the message and the message is strong (e.g. if given by an expert) then the greater the impact. This fits with Milgram's findings — more obedience if the experimenter was an authority figure than if an 'ordinary man' (Experiment 13).

Knowledge check 3

What are two weaknesses and two strengths of agency theory as an explanation of obedience?

Strengths	Weaknesses
The mathematical formula in social impact theory can be applied to all social situations where people are affected by others, so the theory is widely applicable	In social situations it is not that one group impacts on an individual but that there is interaction between the individual and the group. This can be a two-way process
There is reliability in that the formula can be applied over and over and should get the same predictions	There are individual differences that might affect how a social situation affects a particular individual, such as one person being more easily persuadable than another

Table 9 Strengths and weaknesses of social impact theory

Comparing social impact theory and agency theory as explanations of obedience

- Social impact theory is not a theory of obedience alone, whereas agency theory explains obedient behaviour and discusses it directly.
- Social impact theory is more of an explanation than agency theory as it involves a formula that can work in all group situations. Agency theory is rather circular as an explanation because it says people obey authority because they are agents of (they obey) authority.
- Both theories can offer an explanation for Milgram's findings. Social impact theory goes further because it can help to explain the different obedience found if the participant was part of a group (even a group of two).

Factors affecting obedience

Studying Milgram's work on obedience shows that various factors, such as the situation, affect obedience. However, other factors can be looked at as well, including personality, gender and culture.

Personality

In Milgram's (1963) study, 35% of participants did not go to the highest voltage level. Perhaps personality explains this? Personality refers to someone's unique and stable responses to certain situations. There is some evidence that personality can affect whether someone is obedient or not, but the evidence is not clear.

- Elms (1998) analysed the qualitative data from Milgram's work and found a weak link between obedience and occupation. It was thought that occupation might link to personality.
- Using Milgram's data two groups were examined — an obedient group (those who obeyed to the maximum) and a defiant group (those who did not). It was found that the defiant group showed more social responsibility so that might have been a personality trait.
- The defiant group reported more punishment from their parents, so this might have been a reason for not obeying.
- Milgram and Elms (1966) suggested that those who were obedient fitted more into an authoritarian personality.
- Blass found that people who tended to give into authority (high in 'authoritarian submission') tended to be more likely to obey, which supports the idea of personality being a factor.
- Someone who feels in control of their own actions is said to have an internal locus of control. Someone who believes that their actions come from outside themselves has an external locus of control. Blass (1991) reviewed Holland's data (who found no link) and found that internal locus of control linked to resistance to obedience.

Exam tip

You need to learn two theories that can help to explain obedience — social impact theory and agency theory. In your course, when there are two or more theories like this, it is useful to be able to compare and contrast them.

Knowledge check 4

How does social impact theory explain the obedience that Milgram found in his work?

Links

Individual differences link

Individual differences include personality. A particular personality trait might affect obedience. An authoritarian personality might mean more obedience. Someone with an internal locus of control is more likely to resist obedience. However, evidence for personality linking to obedience is not strong.

Issues to show there might be personality differences in obedience	Issues to show there are probably not personality differences in obedience
Elms found some evidence from the interviews of Milgram's participants for there being an authoritarian personality that led to obedience	It is hard to get the evidence for personality as personality was not measured as such in Milgram's work
There is some evidence, according to Blass, that someone with an internal locus of control might be more resistant to obedience	Milgram used a lot of participants and found a high level of obedience, and the level changed as the situation changed. The findings about the situation were secure enough that it was thought unlikely that personality factors alone led to obedience

Table 10 Personality factors as an explanation of obedience

Culture

Milgram's work has been replicated to an extent in different cultures. It is interesting to see whether culture affects obedience — largely the answer is 'no'. If people in different cultures were more or less obedient, it might be said that obedience comes from upbringing. However, if obedience is similar across cultures, then perhaps obedience is in our nature (or, a different explanation, in every culture but learned).

- Meeus and Raaijmaker (1986) partially replicated Milgram's work in the Netherlands (a different culture) and found obedience, as he did.
- Burger (2009) replicated Milgram more exactly, and also found obedience. Burger's study was in the USA as was Milgram's, but it was in 2009 compared with 1963 and there might be cultural differences between the two periods — still obedience was found.
- Blass (2012) reviewed studies of obedience and found that overall in the USA there was 60.94% obedience taking the different studies into account. He compared this figure with the average percentage obedience in other countries, which was 65.94%, and concluded that there was a strong similarity between US obedience and that in other countries.

Links

Developmental psychology link

Obedience seems to be found across cultures. This suggests that obedience is not developed through interaction with the environment, but is 'universal' in our behaviour. 'Universal' means found in all societies and cultures and possibly an evolved trait that supports survival. You can use this evidence to discuss development in humans, to show that some behaviour comes from our genes (possibly a tendency to obey) and some comes from our environment.

Exam tip

If you are doing the A-level, you need to learn about 11 issues and debates, nature–nurture being one of them. You can use evidence for the nature–nurture debate from anywhere in your course, including the idea that obedience to those in authority might be in human nature as agency theory might predict.

Exam tip

When discussing issues in psychology, such as factors affecting obedience, like culture, bring in evidence from studies where possible. Use the evidence without name and date if you cannot remember, but, if possible, use name and date as that is good practice in psychology.

Issues to show there might be cultural differences in obedience	Issues to show there are probably not cultural differences in obedience
There were some differences in obedience levels (though there was agreement that people obey those in authority)	There were differences in the studies' procedures as well as cultural differences, so any difference in findings can be due to study differences
There may be cultural influences in obedience that are not shown by experiments, as they lack ecological validity	The studies had such similar findings that the overall conclusion is that obedience is not down to culture

Table 11 Cultural factors as an explanation of obedience

Gender

Another factor that might explain obedience is gender:

- Milgram did a variation using females and found the same level of obedience in females (65%) as in the males in his 1963 study. It seems there are no gender differences.
- Kilham and Mann (1974) in Australia found gender differences. When administering the shocks 16% of females obeyed to the maximum voltage but 40% of the males did so. When giving orders for someone else to administer the shocks 40% of the females went to the maximum voltage but 68% of the males did so.
- Blass (1991) looked at nine studies, including Kilham and Mann, and found just that one with gender differences.
- Blass (2012) mentions Gupta's (1983) study — in 6 out of 7 conditions in her study, females were found to be less obedient.
- Burger (2009) used both males and females and found similar obedience to Milgram's.
- When the reactions of participants are reported in a study (and that is not always the case) then it is found that there are gender differences in the reactions, with females feeling more anxiety and tension. Females may obey to the same extent, but maybe they feel worse about it.

Issues to show there might be gender differences in obedience	Issues to show there are probably not gender differences in obedience
Kilham and Mann found gender differences, both when the participant administered the punishment and when the participant ordered the punishment, which might give weight to there being gender differences	Milgram did one variation using females and found 65% obedience as with males — there might not be gender differences
Milgram found that female participants reported more tension than male participants in the study	Most of the studies looked at found no gender differences

Table 12 Gender factors as an explanation of obedience

Links

Developmental psychology link

The discussion about whether gender affects obedience can be about development. Gender is both innate in that genes dictate our sex, and learned in that culture 'trains' us to behave in gendered ways. Gender is not found to affect our obedience, which seems to be down to situation and to be universal (found in everyone), however, gender does seem to affect our reaction to going against our morals and enduring stress. Perhaps through social learning and other ways of learning females learn to react with more distress to going against their moral code.

Situation

In Milgram's 1963 study all participants went to 300 volts. It is unlikely that personality was responsible for this obedience, as different personalities were likely to be in the sample. Milgram gave evidence for *situation* being the cause of the obedience when he found lower obedience in a run-down office. There was less obedience when orders were over the phone suggesting removing the presence of the authority figure reduced obedience, again pointing to the situation being the cause of the obedience.

Issues to show there might be situational differences in obedience	Issues to show there are probably not be situational differences in obedience
Many variations were done by Milgram and as he varied the situation obedience changed, which is evidence that the change was down to the situation (all else remained the same)	The problem with using experiments is that they can lack ecological validity, and as 'ecology' is about the situation, this means the findings may not 'fit' real-life situations
Burger (2009) (pages 34–35) replicated Milgram's variations and found similar results, with obedience dropping as the situation changed	It is possible that there were personality factors that gave the changing obedience, such as those with an authoritarian personality being more obedient.So it might not all be down to situation

Table 13 Situational factors as an explanation of obedience

Dissent and resistance to obedience

Obedience can be useful for society, such as soldiers obeying orders to defend their country. However, society might also need people to be autonomous, such as not obeying 'bad' orders and sticking to a moral code. There is interest in dissent and resistance to obedience: 14 out of 40 in Milgram's basic study resisted the orders given.

People resist more when:

- Someone can see the 'victim' (e.g. the victim is in the same room).
- Someone has to be involved directly in the punishment (e.g. holds hand down for a shock).
- Someone is not in a setting that supports authority (e.g. in an office block).
- The one giving the orders is remote (e.g. gives orders over the phone).
- Someone else is seen to resist (e.g. peers rebel).
- There is confusion in the orders, perhaps someone else gives different orders (e.g. more than one experimenter, and one says 'stop').

Exam tip

When discussing resistance to obedience you can use the same evidence as you used to show obedience to authority but focus on the reverse — those who did not obey.

Content: prejudice

You need to know two theories of prejudice — social identity theory (SIT) and realistic conflict theory (or 'realistic group conflict theory', RCT). Factors affecting prejudice and discrimination (personality, situation and culture) are also considered.

- **Prejudice** is an attitude towards other people often based on a stereotype. It involves developing an idea about someone and then carrying that idea forward to apply to all those in that group.
- **Discrimination** is behaviour that arises from prejudice, such as not giving someone a job because of their gender (e.g. thinking females do not make good engineers).

Social identity theory (SIT)

Tajfel and Turner (1979) discuss how prejudice arises from the forming of groups. They suggest that when there are two groups the **in-group** becomes hostile to the **out-group** to protect their own self-esteem. Just having two groups creates prejudice. Social identity is about how people see themselves in relation to membership of their social groups.

- **Social categorisation** is seeing oneself as a member of the group.
- **Social identification** is identifying with the group, taking on the attitudes of the group.
- **Social comparison** is seeing one's own group as better than an out-group, thus maintaining self-esteem.
- These processes lead to in-group favouritism and hostility to the out-group.

Tajfel focuses on how prejudice arises from in-group favouritism, which brings out-group hostility. This leads to discrimination against out-group members.

Tajfel et al. (1970)

Tajfel et al. (1970) carried out experiments in Bristol in the UK to test social identity theory. They showed that people reward their in-group members more than out-group members.

Other studies looking at social identity theory

- Crocker and Luhtanen (1990) found that people who think highly of the group they are in have a high self-esteem as a group and show loyalty to their group.
- Lalonde (1992) found that a hockey team who knew that another hockey team was doing better nevertheless did not admit that the other team was a better team, they said that the other team used 'dirtier' tactics. In this way they could show in-group favouritism.

Strengths	Weaknesses
There is evidence for out-group hostility and in-group favouritism as shown by Crocker and Luhtanen (1990), Lalonde (1992) and Tajfel et al. (1970)	Realistic conflict theory suggests that it is not just having two groups that leads to prejudice and discrimination, but there must also be conflict between them
There are useful applications of the theory. Willetts and Clarke (2013) suggest using the theory to help nurses develop a professional identity, for example	Explaining in-group favouritism as showing how that involves out-group hostility does not take the complexity into account

Table 14 Strengths and weaknesses of the theory of social identity as an explanation of prejudice

Questions & Answers

Social psychology Content Q3 evaluates SIT in more detail.

Realistic conflict theory (RCT)

Realistic group conflict theory is another theory of prejudice. Sherif (1966) is the main name for this theory and his study, the Robber's Cave experiment, is the classic study for social psychology in your course.

Exam tip

When a theory has stages or parts to it, as SIT does, it is useful to learn those stages and to be able to elaborate each stage with an example. Be ready as well to describe just one of the stages/parts.

Knowledge check 5

How would you explain prejudice between two sports teams using social identity theory?

Knowledge check 6

Explain two weaknesses of social identity theory.

Exam tip

Names of researchers in psychology are important and it is useful to use names in the exam. However, if you cannot remember names, then include the material anyway. A 'name' without material will not show knowledge with understanding, but a theory or idea without a name, does show some understanding.

Realistic group conflict theory suggests that whenever there is more than one group in competition over resources there will be prejudice and discrimination. When there is competition over scarce resources in times of hardship then a dominant group shows prejudice towards a weaker group (Filindra and Pearson-Merkowitz, 2013). Duckitt's (1994) work agreed with Filindra and Pearson-Merkowitz (2013) and looked at competition over resources. Resources can be water, food, jobs, territory, financial resources or social resources (e.g. friends). When resources are finite (limited) and there are going to be winners and losers (e.g. over one piece of land), then competition is likely to be more fierce and conflict can last a long time.

Using realistic group conflict theory to reduce prejudice

Practical application of theory is important, as one aim of psychology is to inform society and to improve people's lives. Realistic conflict theory can help to reduce prejudice, such as if the competition over the resources stops, and groups work together to achieve a common overarching goal. See Sherif et al. (1954/1961) for an example of using **superordinate goals**.

Strengths	Weaknesses
The Sherif et al. Robber's Cave experiment was well planned and used good controls. It had good validity too, being a field study, so gives good evidence	The Robber's Cave study starts with two groups who show prejudice even before the competition starts, so there is an element of evidence for social identity theory here
Realistic group conflict theory can help to explain prejudice in many real situations where two groups are in conflict. For example, conflict over land is common (e.g. Palestine-Israel) and conflict over resources/power (e.g. Shiites and Sunni)	In real situations, such as Palestine-Israel, Shiites-Sunni and Ukraine-Russia, it is rare that there is only conflict over one clear resource. Often there is more to it, such as religious beliefs/differences

Table 15 Strengths and weaknesses of realistic conflict theory as an explanation for prejudice

Factors affecting prejudice

A weakness of both theories is that prejudice is complex. Perhaps just saying that prejudice comes from simply being in groups (SIT) or being in competition over scarce resources (RCT) is not enough. There are likely to be other factors involved and in your course personality, situation and culture are considered.

Personality

Personality dimensions often used in social psychology are the 'Big Five'. These are neuroticism, extraversion, conscientiousness, openness to experience and agreeableness.

- Openness to experiences and agreeableness seem to show a negative relationship to prejudice — the more open, and the more agreeable, the less prejudiced.
- Conscientiousness can link to right-wing authoritarianism (see below) and prejudice.

Adorno et al. (1950)

A study by Adorno et al. in 1950 linked an **authoritarian personality** with fascism, which can be seen as an extreme form of prejudice. Authoritarian personalities are rigid thinkers, obedient to authority, see the world as black or white, and stick to social hierarchies and social rules. Right-wing authoritarianism means

Exam tip

Use Sherif et al.'s (1954/1961) study to help to explain realistic group conflict theory. This is the classic study for social psychology in your course.

Exam tip

Use mnemonics to help you learn lists. For example, 'Agreeableness, Conscientiousness, Openness, Neuroticism and Extraversion' can be remembered as 'A CONE' — the first initials of each of the Big Five. You could picture a traffic cone to remind yourself.

authoritarianism linked to political (right-wing) views. Adorno et al. found that those with an authoritarian outlook were more likely to be prejudiced and to show discrimination, especially to those in low-status groups.

Right-wing authoritarianism (RWA) and social dominance orientation (SDO)

- Social dominance orientation means someone who believes in social hierarchy and wants their own group to dominate over others.
- Cohrs et al. (2012) is one of the contemporary studies for social psychology in your course. They found that right-wing authoritarianism showed a relationship with prejudice, agreeing with Adorno et al. (1950). They found openness to experience related to right-wing authoritarianism giving a negative correlation (the more open, the less authoritarian).
- Right-wing authoritarianism is perhaps the opposite of social dominance orientation as it means following rules and obeying orders for the sake of a controlled society. Both can link to being prejudiced.

Links

Individual differences link

A particular personality trait might affect our prejudice and discrimination:
- An authoritarian personality seems to mean more prejudiced (someone authoritarian likes rules, is at odds with their father, chooses a profession with rules, sees the world in black and white, and is a rigid thinker).
- Social dominance orientation (believing in a society with a hierarchy, where people are not all equal) relates to prejudice.
- Openness and agreeableness (two of the Big Five) both relate to prejudice in a negative way — the more open and agreeable, the less prejudiced.
- There does seem to be evidence linking personality to prejudice.

Situation

Guimond et al. (2003) wondered whether the situation might override personality factors as an explanation of prejudice. Levels of prejudice in a society rise and fall over time according to Brown (1995, cited in Akrami et al., 2009), but personality is stable over time, so sudden changes in prejudice seem to be down to the situation at the time. The idea of prejudice coming from a scarcity of resources fits into this idea, as that would be the situation at the time.

Evidence for situational factors in prejudice

- Richard et al. (2003, cited in Akrami et al. 2009) looked at 322 studies and concluded that both situational and personality effects contributed reasonably equally to prejudice.
- Akrami et al. (2009) used RWA, SDO, the Big Five and prejudice as four measures, when they had one group experiencing 'changing norms' experiences and a control group without those experiences. The results were that the situational factor (changing the norm) did affect the level of prejudice, suggesting that situation not personality affects prejudice.

Exam tip

In the issues and debates section of your course (not needed for AS), 'how psychology changes over time' is an issue. Cohrs et al. in 2012 found similar results to Adorno et al. in 1950. Both studies see prejudice as very important and both focus on the authoritarian personality.

Exam tip

If you use acronyms (letters to indicate something, such as RWA for right-wing authoritarianism) then in a piece of writing use the full phrase the first time, with letters in brackets, then use just the letters after that. When revising, keep spelling the whole thing out as well as using the initials — this will help your memory and understanding.

Application of ideas about the situation affect prejudice: reducing prejudice

Allport (1954) suggested that contact can reduce prejudice and there must be:

- Equal status between the people making contact with one another.
- The groups should be working towards a common goal or goals.
- Contact should be harmonious and there should be cooperation.
- Both groups need to acknowledge the authority of the people who have brought them together.
- There should be personal interaction between the people making contact with one another, so that they can learn about one another.
- The contact should occur often and not just in one social situation.
- The minority group members should be seen as typical of their group, not atypical.

There are a lot of situation factors in this list — evidence that situation can lead to prejudice. Situational factors do seem to be involved in prejudice, but personality factors are found as well.

Culture

Research has also looked at whether prejudice can be cultural in cause:

- Cohrs et al. (2012) gathered data in Germany, Adorno et al. (1950) gathered data from Americans, Akrami et al. (2009) worked in Sweden, and Duckitt and Sibley (2010) gathered data in Australia. All these studies looked at RWA, SDO and the Big Five personality dimensions with respect to prejudice and found similar results.
- Pettigrew (1998) looked at whether factors that affect prejudice are different in different countries (Netherlands, UK, France and West Germany) and found universals with regard to what affects prejudice. Pettigrew found similarities in the four countries used.

> **Exam tip**
>
> In the issues and debates section of your course (not for AS) you will see that 'nature-nurture' is an issue. Pettigrew (1998) used data from four different countries/cultures and found similar findings about prejudice, suggesting issues like personality and prejudice are 'universals' (i.e. found in all cultures). This suggests cultural factors (nurture) in prejudice are limited.

- Guimond et al. (2013) thought that cultures with multiculturalism or assimilation in their social norms would show less prejudice than cultures without these features. Multiculturalism (accepting the norms of other cultures all in one country) was seen as high in pro-diversity and assimilation (incorporating other cultures into a country's norms) was seen as low in pro-diversity. Assimilation links to prejudiced attitudes, whereas multiculturalism is more positive about group interactions. The lowest level of prejudice found in Guimond et al.'s (2013) study was found in Canada and the highest in Germany, with the USA and the UK somewhere in between. The researchers found that it was Germany that had the lowest level of norms relating to multiculturalism. If different countries with different pro-diversity policies show different levels of prejudice this suggests that there are cultural factors involved in prejudice.

> **Exam tip**
>
> When explaining a theory or an idea, use examples and evidence. This can help to show understanding.

Links

Developmental psychology link

Culture is learned (relates to our development) in that people pick up on social norms and ideas and these affect the individual's behaviour and attitudes. For example, if a country is multicultural norms will affect policy and members of the society will pick up on such norms (e.g. pro-diversity norms). When Guimond et al. (2013) found that those with multicultural norms were less prejudiced, they were asking about society's norms, which would be learned from the environment such as media and school. This shows that prejudice and discrimination (or lack of prejudice and discrimination) can come from learning and fits within developmental psychology.

Links

Individual differences in obedience/prejudice
- Find the links to individual differences in this section (pages 14 and 19) so you know you are covering this element of your course.

Developmental issues in obedience/prejudice
- Find the links to developmental issues in this section (pages 14, 15 and 21) so you know you are covering this element of your course.

Knowledge check 7

Explain two pieces of evidence that show that culture is a factor in prejudice and discrimination.

Summary

- Obedience is doing what an authority figure says. It can be explained using agency theory: we act as agents of those in authority over us, even if that causes us moral strain. When not in an agentic state, we are in an autonomous state and make our own decisions.
- Obedience can be explained using social impact theory, which considers the role of others in behaviour and in particular attitudes.
- Milgram did a main experiment and found that participants would give what they thought were dangerous levels of shock to someone they thought was another participant. This was a very unexpected finding. When Milgram had asked his colleagues beforehand, they had not predicted the level of obedience he found.
- Milgram did variations and found less obedience in different scenarios, but still found people were willing to give the 'shocks'. It seemed that the less the participant felt they were agents of the authority figure, the lower their level of obedience was.
- Obedience studies raise ethical issues.
- Factors affecting obedience include the situation, as Milgram claimed. Personality too can help to explain obedience to an extent, such as focusing on an authoritarian personality which might show more obedience. Culture and gender seem to be less involved in whether someone shows obedience.
- Studies and theories about prejudice can be used to explain hostility between groups.
- Social identity theory explains that just having an in-group and an out-group can bring about prejudice through various processes.
- Realistic conflict theory suggests that it is not just having groups but having groups in conflict in some way, such as in competition over resources that leads to prejudice and discrimination.
- Personality, situation and culture can be factors that affect prejudice. Though situation is found to be important in prejudice, personality also is important and there are some cultural effects too (unlike findings about obedience).
- There are developmental issues involved in obedience and prejudice, such as culture and gender.
- Individual differences can affect both prejudice and obedience to an extent, but situation is important in obedience. Personality seems to be a strong factor in prejudice, however.

Methods

Before looking at the methods studied in social psychology, some general issues about method need to be considered: why methodology (the study of method) is important and reflect basic methodological features of a study in psychology.

Why methodology is important

Methodology concerns how psychology is carried out — mainly to ensure that results and conclusions are secure. 'Secure' involves various issues that are evaluation points, such as **validity**, **reliability**, **generalisability**, **objectivity**, **subjectivity**, **credibility** — and there are other important evaluation issues, such as ethical issues. To get 'secure' data, the methodology of a study is planned carefully.

Methodology evaluation term	Explanation
Validity	Measuring what you claim to measure, meaning that what you measure is 'real life'
Reliability	Getting the same results if you do a study again, because if you do not get the same results, the data are not worth much
Generalisability	The sampling is such that results can be said to be true of other people that the study is meant to represent
Objectivity/subjectivity	Objectivity means the researcher's own opinions or influences in a study do not cause bias. Subjectivity is when the researcher affects the results with their own views
Credibility	When the results and conclusions of a study are explained, people accept them

Table 16 Key methodology evaluation terms

Basic methodological features of a study

Methodology description term	Explanation
Aim	A brief statement of what the study is intending to find
Hypothesis (alternate)	A carefully defined statement of what the study is aiming to find. The **IV** and the **DV** are both clearly stated, saying exactly what is being done and what is being measured. The social approach talks about the **alternate hypothesis**, which is the overall term for the statement. (There is an **experimental hypothesis** — for experiments — and a **null hypothesis**)
Operationalising	Making something measurable and clear
Independent variable (IV)	The variable that the researcher manipulates (changes) to see the effect on the dependent variable
Conditions	An IV tends to have more than one condition, as it is about the different way that X or Y would affect the DV. There are often two **conditions**, for example, where one condition is the in-group (people in your group) and the other is the out-group (people not in your group)
Dependent variable (DV)	The variable that is measured to see the effect of the IV. In the example about in-group/out-group behaviour the DV was 'act differently', and that would have to be operationalised. For example, saying nice things about the in-group members and unpleasant things about the out-group members, as measured by questionnaire
Control	The IV is changed and the DV measured, but everything else is controlled to make sure nothing else affects the results
Situational variables	Variables in the situation such as noise, temperature and light might affect the results if they are different in the different conditions
Participant variables	Variables in the participants such as mood, hunger, age or gender might affect the results if they are different in the different conditions

Table 17 Key methodology description terms

Research methods

You will cover some main research methods for your AS/A-level course.

Book	Topic area	Main research methods focused on
1	Social psychology	Questionnaires, interviews
1	Cognitive psychology	Experiments (laboratory and field), case studies of brain-damaged patients
2	Biological psychology	Correlational analysis, brain scanning, twin and adoption studies
2	Learning theories	Observations, content analyses and animal experiments

Table 18 Topic areas covered in Book 1 and Book 2 and related research methods

What follows here reflects methods in social psychology.

Self-reporting data: questionnaires

Questionnaires gather **personal data** because the researcher needs to know something about the respondent (the person answering). Only necessary data should be gathered.

Then there are questions that extract the other data required. There are many different ways of asking such questions, such as using a **Likert-type scale** (e.g. strongly agree, agree, don't know, disagree, strongly disagree), or any other **ranked scales**. Questions can simply ask for 'yes' or 'no' answers. Other questions can ask directly for someone's opinion, such as 'What do you think about…?'

Closed questions

Closed questions are those where the answer is a forced choice. An example of a **closed question** is a question asking for the answer 'yes' or 'no'.

Strengths	Weaknesses
Generate standard replies that can be counted for ease of comparability and analysis	Force a choice of answer (even 'unsure') so may not give the answer respondents would prefer, so they are not valid
Same clearly expressed, detailed questions, so if repeated tend to get the same responses; reliable	'Unsure' can mean 'don't know' or 'sometimes yes and sometimes no'; answers may mean different things to different respondents, so they are not comparable

Table 19 Strengths and weaknesses of closed questions

Open questions

Open questions leave the answer open for the respondent to give their views. An example of an **open question** is a question asking 'What do you think about…?'

Strengths	Weaknesses
Respondent is not constrained but free to answer as they wish, so is likely to give more detailed, in-depth and rich data	Difficult to analyse because tend to be interpreted by the respondent, therefore difficult to compare data with those of other respondents
Allows respondent to interpret the questions as they wish, so produces more valid 'real' data than when constrained by the questions	Often are not answered in full as they take longer and it is more difficult to think of the answer than when ticking a forced-choice box

Table 20 Strengths and weaknesses of open questions

Quantitative data

Quantitative data are data where numbers are collected and given scores. For example, if time is measured, that is quantitative. Closed questions gather quantitative data. Even categories like 'strongly agree' involve scoring.

SA: strongly agree; A: agree; DK: unsure; D: disagree; SD: strongly disagree

Statement	SA	A	DK	D	SD
I don't talk much with people outside my own group	5	4	3	2	1
I have lots of friends with the same interests	5	4	3	2	1
I like meeting people even if they are different from me	1	2	3	4	5

The table is scored 'high' for 'prefers own in-group'.

Table 21 Likert-type scale and scoring

Exam tip

You may have to answer the question 'What is meant by quantitative data?' (or *qualitative* data). Often there are 2 or 3 marks available as this is a 'definition' question, so make sure you say enough: you can add an example (which can serve as elaboration), or you can add information to a basic point.

Exam tip

When asked to evaluate methodology, one type of question is to ask for one strength and one weakness, with 2 or 3 marks each. Preparing two strengths and two weaknesses can be useful for a general evaluation question as well, so it is a good study skills habit. Elaborating on each point can gain additional marks.

Exam tip

Examination questions can ask you to make up a question. Practise thinking of an example of both an open and a closed question. For example, ask your friend an open question allowing a free response (such as 'How did you get on last night?') and a closed question (such as 'Did you go to Simon's house last night?').

Qualitative data

Qualitative data are data about opinions and attitudes rather than numbers. They are data that tell a story in some way. Open questions gather qualitative data. For example, 'What do you think of people who do not have the same ideas as you?'

Strengths	Weaknesses
Allow more in-depth analysis because of greater detail	Difficult to analyse because the data can be so different that they are hard to summarise
More valid because respondents can say what they really think	There is more detail and depth and it can take longer both for the researcher and the participant

Table 22 Strengths and weaknesses of qualitative data

A questionnaire usually includes both open and closed questions and so gathers both quantitative and qualitative data. A **pilot study** is useful. This is an initial study run with a few participants to test the questions and check their clarity and suitability. In the light of the pilot, changes can be made.

Exam tip

For terms such as 'open question', 'closed question', 'quantitative data' and 'qualitative data', you may be asked for a definition and/or examples. Using cards or a similar system, practise writing definitions, giving examples, making comparisons between such terms, and giving a strength and weakness, as appropriate. Examples from studies in your course are useful to show course coverage.

Collecting data using questionnaires

Questionnaires can be posted out to people, which can be quite costly and also risks producing a low response rate, but can reach a lot of people. The sample would be a volunteer sample — those who replied. The questionnaires can be handed out by the researcher and completed there and then, handed out by someone else or left somewhere for completion. So this is a flexible research method.

Evaluation of questionnaires as a research method

Here, with regard to questionnaires, evaluation is divided up into issues. This helps to look at the various ways to evaluate covered in your course.

Questions & Answers

Social psychology Method Q1 evaluates questionnaires in more detail.

Evaluate: validity

Questionnaires can be evaluated according to their **validity**, which means how far what they gather is 'real-life' information. Use your textbook or another source to make sure you understand different types of validity.

- **Construct validity:** the questions must do a good job of measuring what they are supposed to measure.
- **Internal validity:** there are no other variables (except the IV) that could have caused the effect.

Knowledge check 9

What is good about qualitative data compared to quantitative data?

Exam tip

Issues used in evaluation — validity, reliability, generalisability, objectivity, credibility and ethics — are useful when evaluating a research method in psychology. To evaluate a study or method, try considering these issues one at a time to generate ideas. They are also key features of psychology that you need to know about.

Exam tip

Questions asking you to evaluate can ask for strengths or weaknesses, or evaluation in general. It is often found that answers giving strengths tend not to gain as many marks as answers giving weaknesses.

- **Ecological validity:** uses the respondent's natural setting.
- **Predictive validity:** results would 'predict' a real-life situation and findings of another study.

Demand characteristics are when characteristics of a question, or features of any study, give clues to the participant about the answer(s) expected.

Social desirability is when people tend to reply as they think they should reply.

Researcher effects is about the characteristics of the researcher, like their age or gender or dress.

Evaluate: reliability

Questionnaires can be evaluated by considering how reliable they are — if the questionnaire were carried out again, would the same results be found?

- Closed questions have forced-choice answers — so are reasonably reliable.
- Questionnaires are set out and repeated exactly — a condition for reliability.
- Open questions allow for opinions to be given — so are less reliable.

Exam tip

Evaluation of one methodological issue can evaluate another. For example, evaluation of closed questions — they yield measurable and replicable answers — can be used to evaluate reliability in questionnaires which use closed questions. Put an evaluation term in the middle of a mind map (e.g. 'reliability') and fill in as many issues about it as possible to form a diagram you can remember.

Evaluate: generalisability

Results are **generalisable** when they come from good sampling that represents the target population, so it can be said that what was found is 'true' of all the others who were not in the sample.

(1) **Random sampling** can give good generalisability because you would expect the sample to be representative of the target population and not to have bias.

(2) **Stratified sampling** can give good generalisability because all the necessary characteristics will be in the sample.

(3) **Volunteer/self-selected sampling** is not easy to generalise from, because there is something different about people who volunteer.

(4) **Opportunity sampling** is not easy to generalise from, because there is no science in how people are obtained and there is a strong element of chance and bias.

Questions & Answers

Social psychology Method Q2 considers problems with sampling.

Exam tip

Four types of sampling can be asked about directly (random, stratified, volunteer and opportunity). Be ready to define any one of these and to discuss them with regards to their generalisability — both how they might give generalisability and how they might not, as well as preparing for other questions about them, such as their strengths and weaknesses.

Exam tip

In a question about validity, you may want to use these different types of validity to extend your answer and add detail. Answers that reach high grades tend to have such detail and use terminology in this sort of way.

Knowledge check 10

What does it mean to say that questionnaires do not measure actual behaviour?

Exam tip

Questions asking about a study or research method can ask you to evaluate in a specific way. Make sure you clearly understand issues like reliability and generalisability. For example, an extended writing/essay question might ask you to describe a study (such as Milgram, 1963) and to evaluate it in terms of reliability and validity.

Strengths	Weaknesses
Low bias because everyone has an equal chance of being chosen	Cannot be certain that the sample is representative of all groups/types etc.
Sample can be checked mathematically for bias	Difficult to access all the population so that random sampling can take place

Table 23 Strengths and weaknesses of simple random sampling

Strengths	Weaknesses
All relevant groups/strata will have at least some representation	It is difficult to know how many of each group is needed in order to represent the target population accurately
Limits the numbers of participants needed	Relies on researchers knowing all the required groups/strata; forces choice of participants and proportions of all groups, so can give bias by excluding people

Table 24 Strengths and weaknesses of stratified sampling

Strengths	Weaknesses
Ethically good because people volunteer, so are willing to be involved	Only certain types of people may volunteer, so there is bias
More likely to cooperate, which means there may be less social desirability and such biases	May take a long time to get enough volunteers

Table 25 Strengths and weaknesses of volunteer sampling

Strengths	Weaknesses
More ethical because the researcher can judge if the participant is likely to be upset by the study or is too busy to take part	Only people available are used and they may be a self-selected group (e.g. not working, so available during the day)
The researcher has more control over who is chosen and should, therefore, be able to get the sample quickly and efficiently	May not get representatives from all groups, so there may be bias

Table 26 Strengths and weaknesses of opportunity sampling

Evaluate: objectivity/subjectivity

Objectivity refers to avoiding bias from the researcher's own opinions and understanding. **Experimenter/researcher effects** must be controlled for, such as the effects of tone of voice, clothes worn or the gender of the researcher. **Subjectivity** is to be avoided when data are gathered as well as when data are analysed.

Evaluate: credibility

Data are credible if they are valid (true to life) and reliable (found more than once). They are credible if they can be generalised (said to be true of others, not just the sample used) and if they agree with common sense.

Evaluate: ethical considerations

In your course, you have studied the BPS Code of Ethics and Conduct (2009) which has four main principles: respect, competence, responsibility and integrity. Questionnaires can have good **ethics**, because ethical considerations can be addressed on the questionnaire itself.

Exam tip

Terms and concepts (e.g. the four types of sampling mentioned here) that are listed in the specification can all be mentioned directly in an examination question. Other terms such as other types of sampling (e.g. snowball sampling, which is finding one participant who then introduces the researcher to others) cannot be asked about directly.

Exam tip

Subjectivity, featuring in social psychology in your course, is about bias in research. The opposite (objectivity) means good science. Try to become familiar with all such terms in the specification because using them appropriately is one way to get a good grade. When doing practice examination questions, aim to use at least one appropriate term in each sentence.

Strengths	Weaknesses
They are often reliable because bias from the researcher can be avoided by having set questions and a set procedure	They could be administered differently by different people, so data may be biased by the situation, which would make them unreliable
If questions and procedure are set so that bias is avoided, data should be valid	If fixed questions are mainly asked, then useful relevant data can be missed, making data invalid. Respondents may not be free to say what they want

Table 27 Strengths and weaknesses of questionnaires

Self-reporting data: interviews

Self-report data, which are data where the respondents give information about themselves, can be collected using interviewing as well as questionnaires. You will have looked at three types of **interviews**.

Type of interview	Explanation	Brief evaluation
Structured	Planned questions throughout	+ Can be repeated and data can be compared – Forced choice, so tends to lack validity
Semi-structured	Themes to be covered are decided but questioning is open	+ More valid, as can explore to get real-life answers – Can be hard to compare data if issues different
Unstructured	Areas planned but questions can follow lead of respondent (looser structure)	+ More valid, as respondent leads – Less comparable and less replicable, so harder to test for reliability

Table 28 Three types of interview

Interviews need a **schedule**, which is the set of questions/areas that need to be covered, whether in a fully structured or unstructured way. There also needs to be a **transcript**, which involves writing out all the replies so that data can be thoroughly and objectively analysed.

When answering questions about interviews, with regard to open and closed questions, qualitative and quantitative data, and analysis of data, use what you have learned about these issues when looking at questionnaires, as the same issues arise. There might, however, be more bias in an interview because the interviewer can feature more, so there might be researcher effects.

Strengths	Weaknesses
Questions can be explained and enlarged upon, so this is a good method when in-depth and detailed data are required	The interviewer may influence the data (e.g. by tone, dress, gender), which would result in researcher bias
Data tend to be valid because interviewees use their own words and are not as constrained by the questions as they are in a questionnaire	Analysis may be subjective (e.g. generating themes) and the researcher's views may influence the analysis

Table 29 Strengths and weaknesses of interviews

Exam tip

Examination questions can ask specifically for evaluation of ethics (of a study), in which case only focus on ethical issues in your answer and be specific. For example, if discussing Milgram's work saying he needed to give the right to withdraw, expand on your answer such as suggesting that in practice participants were pressured by prods to continue.

Knowledge check 11

Write a few sentences that incorporate two ethical issues featured in this section and show clearly what each is and why it is important.

Exam tip

When writing about ethical issues, pay attention to how you word your answer. It is not that participants 'have' informed consent, for example, but that they must 'give' informed consent. Read through your answers about ethics and make sure that the 'name' of the guideline makes sense in a sentence.

Knowledge check 12

Name three types of
interview and give one
strength of each.

Questions & Answers

Social psychology Method Q2d looks at advantages of a type of interview.

Analysis of quantitative data/closed questions

You need to know how to analyse quantitative data including measures of central
tendency (mean, median, mode), measures of dispersion (range, standard deviation)
and graphs (bar charts and frequency tables).

Measures of central tendency

Quantitative data provide numbers. Initial analysis is by means of percentages and
descriptive statistics. Descriptive statistics include **measures of central tendency**,
which are the mode, median and mean average. Graphs are also used, such as bar
charts and you need to know about frequency tables. The data are analysed in such
a way that they can be clearly displayed and understood. Sometimes just totals
are used.

Mode — the most common score in the set of scores:

   1   5   7   8   8   12   12   12   15 — the mode is 12

Median — the middle score in the set of scores:

   1   5   7   8   8   12   12   12   15 — the median is 8

   1   5   7   8   8   11   13   14   15   20 — the median is 9.5 (between 8 and 11)

Mean — the arithmetical average found by totalling all the scores in the set and
dividing by the number of scores in the set:

   1   5   7   8   8   11   13   14   15   20 — the mean is 10.2 (102 divided by 10)

Measures of dispersion

Descriptive statistics also include **measures of dispersion**. The range is a
measure of dispersion, found by finding the highest score or number and taking
away the lowest score, giving the difference between the two — the range of
the scores.

Range — the difference between the top and bottom scores:

   5   7   8   8   12   12   12   15 — the range is 10

Standard deviation is a measure of how far scores vary from the mean average. The
idea is to find the difference of each score from the mean and square that difference
so that minus and plus signs can be ignored. Add up the 'differences squared' for
all the scores and then divide that number by the number of scores minus 1. Then,
finally, find the square root and you have the standard deviation.

$$\sqrt{\left(\frac{\Sigma(x-\bar{x})^2}{n-1}\right)}$$

Exam tip

Using made-up
numbers, practise
working out each of the
measures of central
tendency (mean,
median, mode). Mode
is the fashionable
number (most common),
median is medium (in
the middle), and mean
is meanest (hardest) in
terms of calculations
(add them all up and
divide by the number
there are).

Scores	Difference from the mean	Squaring the difference from the mean
6	0	0
9	3	9
4	−2	4
8	2	4
3	−3	9
Mean = 6		Total = 26
$n − 1 = 4$ (n is number of scores)	SD = 26/4 = 6.5 and then square root = 2.549	
Standard deviation = 2.549		

Table 30 Standard deviation: how far the scores vary from the mean

Knowledge check 13

What is the point of finding the standard deviation of a set of scores?

Exam tip

The maths for calculating standard deviation is not difficult, though it might look hard at first glance. Generate some scores and practise finding the SD a few times. In the exam you are given the formula for calculating the SD.

Graphs

You need to know about bar charts and frequency tables. These are dealt with in this section.

Bar charts

On a bar chart each set of scores is represented by a single bar, such as the mean score for females against the mean score for males. The bars can be displayed horizontally or vertically.

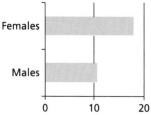

Figure 1 Bar graph showing mean average number of cones hit on a driving course, by gender

Frequency tables

A frequency table shows the number of times a score is found. The usefulness is that the distribution can be seen in table form. Then a histogram (or frequency graph) can be used to display the data.

Table 31 shows the frequency of scores (raw data) from an item on a personality questionnaire asking 20 participants to rate themselves with regard to prejudice on a scale of 0 (not prejudiced) to 5 (self-reported as very prejudiced).

Self-report prejudice score (rating 0 to 5)	Tallying	Frequency of the score
0	–	0
1	11	2
2	111	3
3	̶T̶H̶I̶ 111	8
4	̶T̶H̶I̶	5
5	11	2

Table 31 Raw data showing frequency of scores

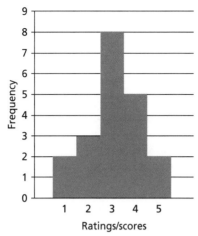

Figure 2 A histogram showing frequency of scores using data from Table 31

Analysis of qualitative data/open questions

Qualitative data are in the form of a story or comments, so need to be summarised to make them manageable and clear. This is done by **thematic analysis**, generating themes from the data. An example might be finding that most respondents on a questionnaire comment on liking people of the same age or on not liking people from a different social class. Themes would be age and class.

Analysis of questionnaires

Using the quantitative data from a questionnaire, scores are assigned to groups obtained from the personal data. For example, scores of males/females, or older/younger people can be separated and compared — depending on the hypothesis/aim of the questionnaire.

The themes from the qualitative data can be sorted into groups such as gender, age or class, depending on what the researcher wants to find out. Perhaps, for example, males talk more about class and females talk more about age.

> **Exam tip**
>
> In methodology questions, you can be asked to apply your understanding to 'unseen' situations. This can include analysing data presented in some format. Make up some data (or use your practical data, so you know what the figures mean). Practise interpretation and analysis. Note trends such as similarities and differences and use actual figures in your answer (percentages or fractions).

> **Knowledge check 15**
>
> Why would qualitative data, from open questions, in their raw form, not be suitable for using descriptive statistics?

Ethical guidelines

All studies need to be assessed for their ethics. This section looks at the BPS Code of Ethics and Conduct (2009) and also at risk management.

> **Exam tip**
>
> You will have learned about measures of central tendency, measures of dispersion and graphs in other subjects. Make a few notes anyway, for revision. Define the terms (use the glossary in this book) and be ready to carry out calculations and draw graphs in the examination.

> **Knowledge check 14**
>
> If one participant comments that they prefer meeting new people and do not see themselves as prejudiced and another comments that they feel that only their group likes them and others are not as nice, find three themes in the data.

> **Exam tip**
>
> Make up some data from a questionnaire (e.g. about obedience), write a short paragraph, then pick out likely themes. It is good to practise analysis as you can be asked to analyse data in the examination. There are no 'right' or 'wrong' themes as long as they come from the data.

The BPS Code of Ethics and Conduct (2009)

There are four principles in this code. They are respect, competence, responsibility and integrity.

Respect

Respect is about researchers being able to explain the ethics of their practice, respecting the dignity of others. Researchers must avoid unfair practices, and must respect others' opinions. Privacy and confidentiality and getting **informed consent** are part of this principle. Respect is about giving self-determination to a participant and includes giving the **right to withdraw** throughout a study.

Competence

A researcher must be competent to carry out a study and must watch for lack of **competence**, taking steps to put that right.

Responsibility

The researcher is responsible for there being no harm or distress. Researchers must also look out for bad practice in other research and must not 'look away'. Where animals are used in research they must be well-treated — there are special guidelines for using when working with animals. **Responsibility** includes **debriefing** at the end of a study, to check any harm done and minimising any difficulties.

Integrity

Integrity is about honesty and accuracy in dealings with others. Results must be published honestly and any conflicts of interest announced clearly. Researchers must keep clear personal boundaries between themselves and the people involved in the study. There must be no **deceit**.

Risk management

There can be risk to participants, researchers, others around or to animals if they are used in a study. There can also be risks to the environment, political risks or risks to society.

Risk must be managed by looking at the highest risk first, working down to the lowest level of threat. It is about looking at the probability of a threat happening against the consequences if it does.

Solutions to manage risk

- Transference of risk means insuring against it happening.
- Mitigation is reducing the risk as far as possible.
- Acceptance might mean budgeting for the risk.

The BPS Code of Human Research Ethics

The BPS Code of Human Research Ethics has a section on management of risk, which states the risk of harm must be no greater than what participants would be exposed to in their 'normal lifestyle'. Use your textbook or another source, like the BPS code which can be found online, to find out more.

Exam tip

Think of ethical guidelines — avoiding deceit, getting informed consent, giving right to withdraw, working within competence and giving a debrief — when assessing studies. Bring in the four principles too — respect, competence, responsibility and integrity — to show understanding of the Code (2009). Draw a diagram to show how these nine terms fit together.

Exam tip

Research can raise ethical and moral issues, e.g. using knowledge of obedience to gain control over a crowd by wearing uniform (social control), and researching in socially sensitive areas, such as prejudice. Risk management is about such sensitive issues. You can use this material when discussing issues and debates in psychology at A-level (not AS).

Knowledge check 16

Why is risk management important when designing a study in psychology?

Summary

- Questionnaires and interviews are popular methods in the social approach and in psychology.
- The two involve the use of open and closed questions, pilot surveys, aims and alternate hypotheses, and, for interviews, interview schedules.
- Interviews can be structured, semi-structured or unstructured.
- With regard to design decisions, open questions gather qualitative data (tend to be more valid) and closed questions (tend to be more reliable) gather quantitative data.
- Quantitative data, which are in the form of numbers, are analysed using descriptive statistics, including measures of central tendency (mode, median and mean) as well as graphs, and measures of dispersion (range and standard deviation).
- Qualitative data, which involve detail in the form of words or pictures, for example, are analysed by thematic analysis, generating themes and categories from the data, grouping comments and ideas to summarise and conclude.
- Both questionnaires and interviews can yield biased data, one aspect being subjectivity as the researcher's views can affect the data. Other bias that both questionnaires and interviews can suffer from include demand characteristics and social desirability, as well as response bias, which affect the validity and reliability of the data.
- All studies in psychology, including those in social psychology, must adhere to ethical guidelines that are laid down by the British Psychological Society (and other bodies). The BPS Code of Ethics and Conduct (2009) has four main sections — respect, competence, responsibility and integrity — and within these issues include getting informed consent, having no deceit, giving the right to withdraw, giving a debrief at the end, and being competent to carry out the study.
- Along with ethical guidelines there must be management of risk.
- A study is generalisable only in so far as the sampling technique reflects the target population, so sampling is important. Four sampling techniques are random, stratified, volunteer/self-selected and opportunity.

Studies

You need to know about the classic study and one of three contemporary studies. The contemporary studies include Reicher and Haslam (2006) and Cohrs et al. (2012), but it is Burger (2009) that is used in this book. You may prefer to revise one of the other two if you studied one of them.

Classic study: Sherif et al. (1954/1961)

The Robber's Cave study (Sherif et al., 1954/1961) is well known. It involves some boys at a summer camp in the USA (Oklahoma) and how prejudice was generated in the camp — also how it was reduced afterwards. Use your textbook or some other source to remind yourself about the aims and procedure of this study.

Results

Stage 1: the groups gave themselves names and norms were developed. Towards the end of this stage they knew about one another and discussed the other group frequently. The existence of an out-group had led to prejudice (as social identity theory would predict).

Stage 2: this came naturally as when they knew about one another they asked to compete. There were negative attitudes towards the out-group. Prejudice had formed due to the competitions.

Stage 3: choice of friends from the out-group at the end of Stage 2 was 6.4% for the Rattlers and 7.5% for the Eagles, similar figures. This shows how much hostility there was at the end of Stage 2. Stage 3, involving them working together to achieve goals, changed this hostility. At the end of Stage 3, choice of friends from the out-group was 36.4% for the Rattlers and 23.2% for the Eagles, showing the reduction in hostility.

Conclusions

- Leader–follower relations developed as a result of having to solve problems through combined action; as group structure stabilised, an in-group formed.
- When two groups meet in competition and in frustrating situations, in-group solidarity and cooperation increases and inter-group hostility is strong.
- Contact between two groups is not enough to reduce hostility.
- When groups needed to work together, exchanged tools, shared responsibilities and agreed how to solve problems, friction was reduced.

Evaluation

Strengths	Weaknesses
There were controls, such as the careful sampling and the briefing of observers so that they followed the same procedures; this meant cause-and-effect conclusions could be drawn	It was unethical in the sense that consent was not obtained, there was no right to withdraw and parents could not visit
There were several data collection methods and the findings agreed, so validity was claimed	It was hard to generalise to other situations because the sample was restricted to boys with a specific background

Table 32 Strengths and weaknesses of the Robber's Cave study by Sherif at al. (1954/1961)

Questions & Answers

Social psychology Studies Q2 assesses the generalisability of Sherif et al.

Contemporary study: Burger (2009)

Burger (2009) did a replication of Milgram's work on obedience. Burger (2009) felt that 150 volts in Milgram's study was the point of no return — those who carried on after this level tended to go to the end. Burger's aim was to replicate Milgram's work ethically, by stopping the study after the 150 volts stage. He also wanted to look at the situation when someone else was there and refused, to see if this meant less obedience. Use your textbook or some other source to revise the study.

Results

Burger (2009) found obedience just as Milgram did, both when replicating Experiment 5 and when doing the other variation.

Conclusions

Burger (2009) felt that the answer to whether the same level of obedience that Milgram found in 1960/1970 was found in 2009. It had been difficult to replicate Milgram's work so that question had not really been answered up to Burger's study. The same situational factors seem to be around today as in the time of Milgram's work.

Exam tip

When revising studies you need to revise the whole study. It is useful to know about report structure: abstract; background/introduction including aims; method (design, participants, materials, procedure); results; discussion (conclusions); references; and to consider studies in terms of these sections. A question can focus on aims, method, results or conclusions rather than the whole study.

Knowledge check 17

Explain how Sherif et al.'s Robber's Cave study supports both realistic conflict theory and social identity theory.

Questions & Answers

Social psychology Studies Q1 explains more about Burger's results and conclusions.

Evaluation

Strengths	Weaknesses
Burger (2009) replicated Milgram's work carefully and even with the differences there for reasons such as ethics, there were considerable similarities. His study can be seen as at least a partial replication and as such reliability can be claimed	Laboratory experiments can lack validity because they take place in an unnatural setting and situation
Ethically the study is strong as Burger takes a procedure that is criticised ethically and makes a lot of changes to make his study acceptable	The conclusion that it was the situation that led to obedience can be criticised if looking at other possible explanations such as looking to the experimenter for norms in a new situation or the experimenter taking responsibility

Table 33 Strengths and weaknesses of Burger's (2009) partial replication of Milgram's work

Exam tip

Use Burger's study when discussing factors affecting obedience such as situation, personality, culture and gender. Also his study can be used to evaluate Milgram's work. Burger used random allocation to groups so is an example of that methodology, and is also an experiment.

Knowledge check 18

Using Burger (2009) and Sherif et al. (1954/1961), briefly compare their research methods.

Summary

- Sherif et al. (1954/1961), the classic study in social psychology in your course, wanted to study how prejudice starts, is maintained and might be overcome.
- The study looked at boys in a summer camp in the USA, and how prejudice was generated in the camp — also how it was reduced afterwards.
- Burger (2009) is a contemporary study in social psychology in your course. Burger wanted to
- replicate Milgram's work in the 1960s and 1970s in an ethical way.
- The results matched Milgram's findings from Experiment 5 and his findings with regard to the variation. Burger confirmed Milgram's conclusion that obedience comes from a situation (and not from personality, gender or culture).

Key question

You need to know about one key question which social psychology concepts and research can explain. The question must be important to today's society. One key question is looked at in this book, however, you may have studied another one and might prefer to revise that one.

How can prejudice in situations such as crowd behaviour or rioting be reduced?

Describing the question

- Football hooliganism is a well-documented social phenomenon that occurs from time to time and in different countries. In 2013 during a Russia cup game there was violence from football fans, so the issue is a contemporary one. This is an issue for society as policing crowds costs money and when people are hurt and need care, there are costs.
- Rioting is crowd behaviour that is out of control — such as looting in shops or setting cars alight. In Tottenham in 2011 a crowd gathered and then became violent, with rioting. Buildings were set alight, shops were ransacked. There were people hurt, both rioters and police, with inevitable costs for society (financial and emotional costs).
- The question is how such behaviour can be reduced, to reduce the costs to society that have been outlined.

Concepts, theories and research from social psychology in your course

Explaining football fan and crowd behaviour using theories and concepts

- With regard to football hooliganism, two groups of supporters can easily identify each other. This makes identification with an in-group stronger, which is likely to mean that prejudice against the out-group is also strong. These concepts are from social identity theory. Social identity theory suggests that people identify with their in-group and think of their group as being superior because this enhances their self-esteem. They see the members of the other group as inferior, which can lead to prejudice and hostility.
- Realistic group conflict theory is another explanation which suggests that when teams compete, they are likely to be prejudiced against one another. Football is all about competition. The claim of social identity theory that just having two groups causes prejudice might not explain football violence — it could be about competition. Realistic group conflict theory might also help to explain riot behaviour where there is looting of shops and stealing of goods, as this might show competition for resources in times or places of economic hardship.
- Realistic conflict theory suggests that one way of reducing prejudice is to have two groups work together towards a goal that they both aspire to. This could explain why, when thinking about controlling football hooliganism, supporters of two opposing UK teams might come together as supporters of their national team.
- Sherif at al. (1954/1961) found that prejudice was reduced between two groups of boys who had built up rivalry and prejudice when the boys had to work together towards what was called a 'superordinate' goal. Crowd rioting could be calmed if the crowd had to work towards a common goal (e.g. a crowd needing to save their neighbourhood from complete destruction).

Questions & Answers

Social psychology Key questions Q1 and 2 explain more about this section.

Exam tip

List concepts from what is given here (e.g. the social identity theory of prejudice) and use them to explain another key question, such as soldiers 'just following orders'. You will find that the concepts and ideas you have studied will be useful in explaining many questions/issues.

Knowledge check 19

Choose a key question to prepare for the exam and give at least four points of description of this issue.

Summary

- A key question that relates to social psychology is something that society wants explaining or dealing with and an issue involves a question more than a statement, for example 'what is the explanation for...'.
- One key question is how to reduce rioting and football fan violence, which costs society in terms of money and emotions.
- Football fan violence can come from teams seeing themselves as the in-group and the other team as the out-group, hence there is hostility as social identity theory predicts. Changing the in-group to incorporate both groups (such as both love football) might help to reduce the prejudice and help society.
- Rioting behaviour can come from two opposing groups (e.g. policy and a crowd with a grievance) and social identity theory can be useful in this situation too. Realistic group conflict might explain the behaviour as rioters' grievance can often relate to inequality in terms of share of society's resources.
- Sherif et al.'s (1954/1961) study is useful to explain realistic conflict, both how prejudice arises and how it can be reduced.
- Milgram (1963 and his variations) and Burger (2009) can help with suggestions about how to gain control through gaining obedience.

Practical investigation

You will have carried out at least one practical within social psychology, which will have been a questionnaire. Go back over your notes to revise what you did, as it is not possible here to help you to revise that part of the course.

Some general ideas about the practical and what to learn

Make sure you know about:

- qualitative and quantitative data and how you gathered both types of data
- the aims of your study
- how you drew up the questionnaire
- what type of sampling you used and why
- how to use techniques such as Likert-type questions to gather data
- what personal data are and why they are needed
- what is meant by standardised instructions and why they are important
- how to analyse quantitative data in terms of numbers and percentages, including bar charts, frequency tables, mean, median, mode, range and standard deviation
- how to analyse qualitative data in terms of generating themes
- ethical issues you addressed, and perhaps any ethical issues you could not address, including management of risk
- issues you controlled, such as how the questions were asked or having the same standardised instructions — and perhaps issues you could not control
- the independent variable and dependent variable if appropriate
- conclusions that you drew
- how to write up the procedure, results and discussion sections

Questions & Answers

Social psychology Practical investigation Q1 explains more about this section.

Exam tip

Look at past papers to see the format of questions about practical investigations. The AS sample assessment materials, available on the Edexcel website, have an example. There is no guarantee about the format of such questions but it would be a good idea to use your own practical investigation to prepare answers to questions that have already been asked.

Knowledge check 20

With regard to your practical in social psychology, explain your sampling technique (how did you find your participants?) and one way in which you dealt with an ethical guideline.

Content Guidance

Summary

- Revise the practical that you carried out as you will be asked information about what you did and what you found, for example.
- The practical must have used a questionnaire.
- You must have gathered qualitative and quantitative data and be able to talk about both.
- Make sure that your work is ethical and that you can answer questions about the ethics of your work.
- Design decisions include the planning of the questionnaire (e.g. standardised instructions, what questions are asked and reasons for choosing them), what ethical issues there are, considering a pilot study, thinking about any controls necessary and choosing the type of data (qualitative and quantitative), with reasons for your choice.
- Sampling decisions are important, including who the participants were and how they were found.
- Prepare an analysis of both the qualitative and quantitative data as well as brief conclusions about the findings and the area of the study.

Issues and debates (A-level only)

If you are studying for the AS, you do not need to know about issues and debates.

To help A-level students to become familiar with the 11 'issues and debates' ready for their Topic 9 section, they are explained at the end of each topic area and they are reviewed here with social psychology in mind.

Issues and debates in psychology	Links to social psychology in your course
Ethical issues in research	Milgram's ethics have been discussed as having strengths and weaknesses and Burger's replication responds to ethical criticisms of Milgram. The BPS Code of Ethics and Conduct (2009) and the BPS document about risk management are important.
Practical issues in research	Studies show the importance of practical issues such as choosing samples for two conditions in an experiment (Burger, 2009, and Sherif et al., 1954/1961).
Reductionism	When prejudice is measured by questionnaire items this can reduce the complexity of attitudes and behaviour to something measurable, which is useful. However, the validity of using such reduction is questionable.
Explaining using different themes	Social identity theory and realistic conflict theory use different themes and concepts to explain prejudice.
Psychology as a science	Milgram uses laboratory experiment procedures, including controls over variables and careful manipulation such as just changing where the orders are given from.
Cultural and gender issues in research	Obedience is found not to be affected by gender or culture by most studies. Culture might affect prejudice though, at least to an extent.
Nature-nurture	As prejudice links to both right-wing authoritarianism and social dominance orientation in most studies, no matter which country they are carried out in, this suggests that prejudice is more in the situation and a universal rather than being something we learn from our environment. Personality, which is different in individuals, might be 'nature'.
Development over time	Milgram worked in the area of obedience in the 1960s and 1970s. Burger replicated Milgram's work and his findings in 2009 to take into account revised ethical principles over the time, so current practice is not dissimilar to practice in the middle of the twentieth century. Cohrs et al. (2012) examined how personality traits such as the authoritarian personality relate to prejudice, just as Adorno et al. did in 1950.

Issues and debates in psychology	Links to social psychology in your course
Social control	Obedience findings can be used as a form of social control, such as people being manipulated into obeying when someone puts on a uniform or says they have authority.
Use of psychology within society	The key question shows how psychology is used within society.
Socially sensitive research	Prejudice can be socially sensitive. When a study finds less prejudice in a multicultural society like Canada and more in a less multicultural society like Germany, this can be socially sensitive information as prejudice links to racism.

Table 34 Issues and debates and how social psychology illustrates each

Exam tip

The 11 issues and debates are repeated at the end of each topic area to show how that topic area illustrates them. Make notes for each issue and debate, drawing together all the ideas in the topic areas, so that you have a wide range of examples of that issue/debate.

Summary: social psychology

After studying this topic area, you should be able to understand, apply and comment on:

- two theories as they relate to obedience — agency theory and social impact theory
- Milgram's research in obedience including his original (1963) study and three specific variations (Experiments 7, 10 and 13)
- factors affecting obedience and dissent/ resistance to obedience including personality (individual differences), gender, situation and culture
- two theories of prejudice — social identity theory and realistic conflict theory
- factors affecting prejudice including personality, situation and culture
- issues around individual differences and development within obedience and prejudice
- methods gathering self-report data — questionnaires and interviews
- four sampling techniques (random, stratified, volunteer and opportunity)
- ethical guidelines in psychology in the BPS Code of Ethics and Conduct (2009) and risk management
- Sherif et al. (1954/1961) as the classic study and Burger (2009) as the chosen contemporary study (you may wish to revise a different contemporary study)
- one key question relating to the material in social psychology in your course
- one practical investigation that you have done while studying this topic area
- if you are studying A level, issues and debates reflected in social psychology in your course

■ Cognitive psychology

This section looks at cognitive psychology. For some areas you can choose what you study. In this section suitable material is presented, but you may have studied different examples. *You might be better advised to revise the material you chose for your course.*

Content
Four theories of memory are covered: the working memory model, the multi-store model, episodic/semantic memory and the theory of reconstructive memory. Individual differences and developmental issues in cognitive psychology covered in your course also need to be considered.
Methodology
The method covered is experiment, both field and laboratory and related issues such as hypotheses and variables. Inferential statistics are covered, including the Wilcoxon and Mann–Whitney U-tests. A case study of brain damaged patients is covered, including HM.
Two studies in detail
Baddeley (1966b) as the classic study, and Sebastián and Hernández (2012) as the contemporary study are given. You may have covered Schmolck et al. (2002) or Steyvers and Hemmer (2012) instead.
Key question
The chosen key question is how psychologists' understanding of memory can help patients with dementia. You may have looked at one or more different key questions.
Practical Investigation
You will have carried out at least one practical within cognitive psychology and you should use your own practical, which is 'learning by doing'. Some ideas about the practical are suggested in this book.
Issues and debates*
Unless you are studying at AS, there are 11 issues and debates in your course: ethics; practical issues in the design and implementation of research; reductionism; comparisons of ways of explaining behaviour using different themes; psychology as a science; culture and gender; nature-nurture; understanding of how psychological understanding has developed over time; issues of social control; the use of psychological knowledge in society; and issues related to socially sensitive research.
*Issues and debates are not required at AS, but they can be useful for evaluation purposes.

Table 35 Summary of cognitive psychology in your course

The cognitive approach is about what happens to information that comes in through the senses, including how it is processed in the brain. The multi-store model is an example of **information processing**. There is input, some processing occurs, and then there is output.

The cognitive approach has also used the idea of the brain being like a computer — which has input, processing and output. Using the **computer analogy**, ideas can be suggested for how processing takes place.

Questions & Answers

Cognitive psychology Overview Q1 explains more about cognitive psychology.

Exam tip

Use this table to draw up a checklist of what you need to cover. Annotate it to show what you feel you know, what just needs some brief revision and which areas you need to focus on.

Content: four memory models

You need to know four theories of memory: the working memory model; the multi-store model; episodic and semantic memory; and the reconstructive model of memory. These are covered in this section.

The multi-store model of memory (Atkinson and Shiffrin, 1968)

The multi-store model of **memory** illustrates how cognitive psychology is about information processing. Memory involves:

- **encoding** information, which means it is in a particular form
- **storage**, which means how it is kept
- **retrieval**, which is how we remember

The multi-store model focuses on these issues as well as **capacity**, which is how much information can be stored, and **duration**, which is how long it can be stored for. In the multi-store model there are three stores.

The first store is the **sensory register**, where information comes in from the senses:

- Capacity is unlimited in one sense as all information arrives at the sensory register.
- Duration is up to 2 seconds.
- **Mode of representation** is **modality specific** (information is in the same form as it is received).

The second store is **short-term memory** (STM). If there is rehearsal of information in short-term memory then that information goes into long-term memory, otherwise it is lost:

- Capacity is limited to between 5 and 9 chunks or items of information.
- Duration is up to 30 seconds.
- Mode of representation is auditory.

The third store is **long-term memory** (LTM):

- Capacity is potentially unlimited.
- Duration is potentially unlimited.
- Mode of representation is semantic (relies on meaning) but can also be visual or acoustic.

Exam tip

Questions about topic areas themselves, such as social and cognitive psychology, and what they are, can be asked in your examination papers. Be ready to write not only about specific content within an approach but also about the approach itself.

Knowledge check 21

Define cognitive psychology, including two examples.

Strengths	Weaknesses
Experiments such as the one by Glanzer and Cunitz (1966) support the model because it explains primacy and recency effects. They found the first words in a list are remembered, are rehearsed and go into LTM, and the last words are remembered, they are still in STM. The middle words are lost	The experiments that give evidence for the model use artificial tasks so might not be valid
Case studies such as that of HM support the model; they give physiological support, e.g. the hippocampus may be an area for short-term memory	The working memory model shows that STM is more complex

Table 36 Strengths and weaknesses of the multi-store model of memory

The working memory model (Baddeley and Hitch, 1974)

Working memory is the study of short-term memory. It looks at how short-term memory is used and how it works. The working memory model is a system between perception (information coming into the brain) and long-term memory. Baddeley is interested in this not only as a model (a proposal about how things work) but also as a biological system in the brain.

Baddeley and Hitch's (1974) original three-component model of working memory has the following components:

- a **central executive** that supervises the system and controls the flow of information
- a **phonological loop** that holds sound information (split into the **articulatory loop** for speech, e.g. using rehearsal in memory) and the **primary acoustic store** (for auditory information)
- a **visuospatial sketch pad** that deals with visual and spatial information

Baddeley found that people could not do two tasks that used visual or auditory processing as well as they could do two tasks, one involving visual processing and one processing sound, so he came up with the idea of one component dealing with sound and one with vision. The central executive is there to explain how such processing is controlled.

Strengths	Weaknesses
There is evidence for the model — for example, simultaneously carrying out two tasks involving sound is difficult	The model has been added to to take account of results from new studies, e.g. adding the episodic buffer; therefore, the original model was inadequate
The model has generated research, including linking with neuropsychological research	Studies testing the model use experiments with artificial tasks, so results may lack validity

Table 37 Strengths and weaknesses of the working memory model of memory

Links

Developmental psychology link

Children with dyslexia can have their memory span affected. This can affect their learning and development (according to short-term memory the span is about 7 items, which can be enhanced by chunking, and dyslexia can affect such processing). Also dyslexia can affect working memory, so models of memory can help in understanding and helping a child's development.

Questions & Answers

Cognitive psychology Content Q1 compares the multi-store and working memory models.

Episodic and semantic memory (Tulving, 1972)

Long-term memory can be split into **episodic** and **semantic** memory, which links to the multi-store model. Tulving points out that a lot of memory categories have been suggested (e.g. sensory, short-term, long-term, working, semantic, visual, auditory and reconstructive). Many of these types of memory fit into either short- or long-term memory.

Exam tip

You can use the ideas from the multi-store model for your revision. Use short lists of material and short sessions — and rehearse the material well, so that the middle information is not lost (Glanzer and Cunitz, 1966), for example.

Exam tip

When revising use chunking, such as 'GRAVE' for evaluation of studies (generalisability, reliability, application, validity, ethics), to take into account that STM has a capacity of around seven items.

Exam tip

There are a lot of terms in the working memory model. Remembering them will help you to write about the model in an examination. Use the terms to take you through how the model works. Draw a diagram of the model, using the terms, from memory, to check your understanding.

Knowledge check 22

Give two similarities and two differences between the multi-store and working memory models of memory.

It is semantic memory (semantic = meaning) that Tulving focused on. Tulving suggested that in what is thought of as semantic memory, there is memory for episodes in our lives. Semantic memory is about giving meaning to things, and episodic memory is autobiographical, being memories about the individual.

Strengths	Weaknesses
There is neurophysiological evidence for the model — episodic memories seem to be affected if there is medial temporal lobe or prefrontal lobe damage, different from semantic memories	The model is more descriptive than explanatory — labelling memory for events and what happens to us as 'episodic' and memory for what things mean as 'semantic' — rather than explaining memory in detail
Tulving explains in a lot of persuasive detail about the two types of long-term memory, such as how semantic memories can be created using other semantic memories (without stimulation from external stimuli) whereas episodic memories have to be encoded and stored individually	The two stores do rely on one another and are hard to separate — the meaning of the list of words and the 'episode' of learning them are not that easy to separate as you can add meaning by adding information about the act of learning

Table 38 Strengths and weaknesses of the episodic and semantic distinction in memory

Links

Developmental psychology link

Developing our episodic memories (as well as semantic memories) through our experiences is a way of understanding an individual's memories. The importance of developmental influences on memory can be used to help those with dementia as their episodic memories can be triggered if relevant stimuli are present in their environment, which can be helpful for them.

Reconstructive memory (Bartlett, 1932)

Bartlett was a well-known psychologist and his work is still used and respected today. He made famous the idea that memory is not a completely accurate recording of what happens in life. He said we have **schemata**/schemas — plans and information about things that we have already learned or assumed. We process information through these schemata without knowing it. This means our memories are affected and what we recall is not 'pure' information. Memory is reconstructed.

In his 'War of the Ghosts' story study, Bartlett (1932) found that participants added to the story so that it made sense to them, which he called **confabulation**. They altered some important parts to fit their own schemata too, which he called **rationalisation**. And when he asked them to remember it again, after a short while, they recalled less. Using this story, he showed that people reconstructed the story so that it made sense and to fit their schemata.

Strengths	Weaknesses
There is much evidence for the theory: Bartlett (1932) and the work of Loftus on eyewitness testimony	Bartlett's (1932) story did not make sense so participants may have altered it because of demand characteristics
The theory can be tested experimentally	The theory describes memory as reconstructive but does not deal with the processes

Table 39 Strengths and weaknesses of the theory of reconstructive memory

Content Guidance

Questions & Answers

Cognitive psychology Content Q2 and Q3 focus on models of memory.

Links

Individual differences link

Memory, according to reconstruction theory, is not like a tape recorder. We would not expect witnesses to a car accident to remember the event in the same way. Each of us has our own schemas, built through experiences with the environment and schemas (or schemata) affect our recall of events. There are individual differences in memory which can come from our speed of thinking or how we encode memories.

Links

Developmental psychology link

Developing our understanding of the world through schemas is an explanation that fits the reconstructive theory of memory.

Links

Individual differences in memory

Find the links to individual differences in this section (page 44) so you know you are covering this element of your course.

Developmental issues in memory

Find the links to developmental issues in this section (pages 42–44) so you know you are covering this element of your course.

Exam tip

You may be asked to compare theories of memory. Comparing implies explaining both similarities and differences. Making a list of points of similarity and difference is a good way of understanding theories, so is a useful task when revising. Draw up tables, e.g. for comparing methods and comparing studies.

Knowledge check 23

If experiments are used and their findings back up a theory, what is the advantage of using the experimental method rather than a different method?

Summary

- The multi-store model of memory has three stores — the sensory, the short-term store and the long-term store.
- Working memory studies suggest there are different processes in short-term memory, including a central executive to control the processing.
- Episodic and semantic memory are two types of long-term memory — episodic being about events that have happened to us and relate to us (autobiographical) and semantic being memory for meanings such as meaning of words.
- Reconstructive memory is another theory of memory, linked to Bartlett. The theory suggests that memory is not like a recording, it is reconstructed (and so not faithful to reality).
- Bartlett carried out a study using the 'War of the Ghosts' story and showed that when people did not have clear schemas for what was being encoded, they changed bits to suit their own schemas (rationalisation).
- Reconstructive memory is a useful theory to refer to when explaining how an eyewitness is not likely to give a completely accurate (as if recorded) account of what they see.

Method

For what you need to know regarding method in cognitive psychology use Table 35 (page 40).

Table 40 lists what you should already know if you have studied the social psychology part of this book. Check that you understand each of these methodological issues.

Page reference	Feature of experiments
22	Alternate hypothesis
22	Independent variable (IV)
22	Dependent variable (DV)
22	Operationalisation
22	Control
22	Situational variables
22	Participant variables
22	Condition
22	Objectivity/subjectivity
22	Reliability
22	Validity
26	Experimenter/researcher effects
22	Generalisability
22	Credibility
26	Demand characteristics

Table 40 Methodological issues within cognitive psychology covered already in this book

There are also other features of experiments that you need to know about. They are explained here.

Laboratory experiments

- These are experiments carried out in an artificial controlled setting, such as a laboratory. The main feature is control and the setting is an unnatural one for the participants because of this control.
- The independent variable (IV) is manipulated in some way. The dependent variable (DV) is recorded.
- Participant and situational variables would be controlled in a laboratory experiment.
- The aim of a **laboratory experiment** is to find a cause-and-effect conclusion so that scientific knowledge can be built.

> **Exam tip**
>
> The IV usually has two parts to it — the two conditions of the study. For example, one group of participants is given words with a theme and the other words with no theme. The IV is 'whether the words have a theme or not', not just 'theme'. A good tip is not to give one-word answers for the IV.

> **Questions & Answers**
>
> Cognitive psychology Method Q1 gives information on experiments that can help.

> **Exam tip**
>
> The specification splits methodology up so that each approach includes some important methodological issues. However, in reality methodological issues will be repeated. Repetition aids recall, so the more you look again at methodological terms such as those listed here, the more you will understand them. Practise explaining the terms in Table 40 to someone else (or imagine doing that).

> **Knowledge check 24**
>
> Give one example of a situational variable and one of a participant variable.

> **Exam tip**
>
> The DV is what is measured in a study. In the example given here, the researcher thinks more of the words will be recalled if there is a theme, and is measuring the number of words correctly recalled from the list, which is the DV. With the DV, also avoid one-word answers (such as 'recall').

Content Guidance

Field experiments

These are experiments carried out 'in the field', which means in the participants' natural setting. This can be, for example, a hospital (for doctors, nurses or patients). The main feature is the natural setting, together with the controls of a laboratory experiment, though these may be difficult to put into place.

Apart from the natural setting, **field experiments** have the same features as laboratory experiments, including IV, DV, controls and aiming for cause-and-effect conclusions.

Laboratory	Field
Good controls; replicable; reliability can be tested	More ecologically valid than laboratory experiments because they take place in natural settings
Good controls; cause-and-effect relationship can be established	Fairly replicable because of experimental features

Table 41 Strengths of the two different types of experiment

Laboratory	Field
So controlled that tasks may not give valid results because they are not natural/real	Natural setting, so hard to control all factors, which means results may be less valid
Environment unnatural and controlled, so not ecologically valid	Hard to control because of natural setting, so may not be replicable
Experimenter effects can mean results are not valid because there may then be bias	Experimenter effects can mean results are not valid because there may then be bias

Table 42 Weaknesses of the two different types of experiment

Features of research methods

As well as the list of features of research methods in Table 40, you also need to know about other features.

Experimental and null hypotheses, directional or not

- In most studies there is a hypothesis (though there are exceptions, as in case studies, which you will study later in your course).
- A hypothesis is a statement of what is expected.
- There is a **null hypothesis**, which is the one that is tested, and which you will learn more about later in this section.
- There is the **alternate hypothesis** — the alternative to the null — that there is a difference as predicted, as you saw in the method section in social psychology (page 22).
- In an experiment, the alternate is the **experimental hypothesis**.

Hypotheses: directional or non-directional

- A **directional hypothesis** means that the direction of the difference is predicted, e.g. one list is *better* remembered.
- A **non-directional hypothesis** is where the direction is not predicted, e.g. there is different recall from the two lists.
- For information, 'directional' relates to 'one-tailed' and 'non-directional' relates to 'two-tailed'. This is discussed more when inferential statistics are looked at.

Knowledge check 25

Give two differences and two similarities between a field experiment and a laboratory experiment.

Exam tip

If revision time is short, learning strengths and weaknesses of the different types of experiment can help in understanding what the two types are and describing them accurately (e.g. a weakness of a field experiment is that it is hard to control variables because the setting is naturally occurring — this tells you what a field experiment is).

Exam tip

Read exam questions carefully. For example, 'a field experiment' in the question 'What is one strength of a field experiment?' can imply 'the field experiment as a research method' or 'a field experiment that has been carried out'. Look for words that focus the question, for example 'What is one strength of a field experiment as a research method'.

Methodology questions often involve knowing the IV and the DV, considering controls, knowing the experimental design of the study or giving a hypothesis — often specifically asked for as directional (one-tailed) or non-directional (two-tailed). So be ready to answer such questions by making up a short study or using past papers to do so and then considering the methodological issues involved.

Experimental/research designs

There are three **experimental designs**, sometimes called **participant** or **research designs**. There are only three ways of sorting participants into groups to study them.

- **Independent groups design** means to have different participants for each condition.
- **Repeated measures design** means that all the conditions involve the same participants.
- **Matched pairs design** means different participants in the conditions, as in an independent groups design. But the participants are matched so that the two groups have 'as if' the same people.

Repeated measures	Independent groups	Matched pairs
Participant variables are controlled because all participants do all conditions	No order effects to affect results	Helps to control participant variables
Uses fewer participants, so more efficient in terms of cost, convenience and ethics	Demand characteristics less likely	No order effects

Table 43 Strengths of the different participant designs

Repeated measures	Independent groups	Matched pairs
Order effects such as practice and fatigue effects can affect the results if there is no counterbalancing	Participant variables may affect the results	Different people are used, so there may be participant variables that affect the results
Demand characteristics are possible because participants could guess the aim(s) of the study	More participants are needed, so less efficient and less ethical	More participants are needed, so less efficient in terms of cost and less ethical

Table 44 Weaknesses of the different participant designs

Questions & Answers

Cognitive psychology Issue and debates Q1 discusses practical issues in design decisions.

Extraneous and confounding variables

Extraneous variables are those that must be controlled in a study. If they are not controlled they can be confounding variables. **Confounding variables** are things that may well have caused the results other than what was manipulated. Extraneous variables are those that have to be controlled or might not be able to be controlled such as the mood the participants are in.

Give a directional experimental hypothesis for a study looking at whether boys in the playground are more aggressive/rough than girls.

For each of the three designs, what is one study you could make up that the design could be used for and why?

Tables that summarise strengths and weaknesses help revision. However, make sure that for each short summary point you are able to expand it fully to make it clear. Take one or two of the points in the table here and write them out in sufficient detail that you could get 2 marks, for example.

Counterbalancing, randomisation and order effects

If the same people do all the **conditions** they may well get practised and get better (**practice effect**), or get tired and get worse (**fatigue effect**). These two situations are called **order effects**, as they are due to the order in which the conditions are carried out.

There are two ways of avoiding order effects in a repeated measures design. One is to **counterbalance**, which means alternating the order in which the participant does the conditions. The other way is called **randomisation**, which means choosing the order in which the participant does the conditions, for example by tossing a coin.

Order effect/issue	What it means
Practice effect	Having done one of the tasks (conditions), the participant does the next one better because of having had practice
Fatigue effect	Having done one of the tasks (conditions), the participant does the next one less well because of being tired
Counterbalancing	Alternating the order in which the tasks are presented, to counteract order effects. If the first participant does task A then task B, the next does task B then task A
Randomisation	Choosing at random which task the participant will do first. This can be done by tossing a coin (e.g. heads it is task A first)

Table 45 Order effects and how to deal with them

Analysis of quantitative data (non inferential)

Analysis of quantitative data has been covered in the social psychology part of this book (pages 29–31).For the cognitive psychology topic area what you need to know is not covered here, but is listed in Table 46 to remind you. Check that you understand each of the features listed here.

Page number	Feature
29	Measure of central tendency — mean
29	Measure of central tendency — median
29	Measure of central tendency — mode
29	Measure of dispersion — range
29	Measure of dispersion — standard deviation
30	Frequency tables
31	Histogram

Table 46 Analysis of quantitative data required in cognitive psychology covered already in this book

Normal and skewed distribution

It is useful to know whether the way scores in a data set are distributed around the mean average is **normal** or skewed. With normally distributed data the mean, median and mode are more or less the same. If the median/mode are different from the mean average, data will be **skewed**. This is important when it comes to statistical testing as to use some of the tests data must be normally distributed. Also, sometimes an **outlier** score will be discounted when doing an analysis of the data as an outlier affects the mean average and will change the result of the statistical test.

Knowledge check 28

What are two ways of avoiding order effects?

Exam tip

The glossary includes many methodology terms. Work through it picking out the methodology terms, make a list and then check that you can define all the terms and use them. Index cards might be a good way of revising, with the methodological term on one side and explanations and examples on the other.

Exam tip

Frequency tables and histograms were discussed on pages 30–31. The example there showed normal distribution and a 'normal curve'. Make up some data, use the mean, median and mode to see if they seem to be normally distributed. Then use a frequency table and histogram to see whether they are normally distributed. This will help in understanding this issue of distribution.

Cognitive psychology Method Q2b is about normal distribution of scores.

Analysis of quantitative data (inferential testing)

In cognitive psychology you need to know about two statistical tests — the Mann–Whitney U-test and the Wilcoxon signed rank test — and about general issues when using statistical testing, including probability and levels of significance, observed and critical values, and sense checking of data. You need to know about one- and two-tailed when it comes to using statistics tests, about Type I and Type II errors and about normal and skewed distribution. These issues are reviewed briefly in this section.

The four inferential tests in your course

You need to know about the Wilcoxon and the Mann–Whitney U tests in cognitive psychology, but it is worth looking at all four of your tests in this table, to help your learning .The four inferential tests you need to know about are the **Spearman, Mann–Whitney U, Wilcoxon,** and **Chi-squared**. Table 47 shows which test is used in which circumstances — you can see more about what 'nominal, ordinal and interval' mean later in this section (these are levels of measurement). Use the table to give reasons for using the test as well as to find out which test to use. AS students do not need to know this directly, but it can be useful to know why you are using different tests in your practical investigations.

Test of difference			
	Nominal data only	Ordinal data (or interval data)	Interval data only
Repeated measures or matched pairs	Not required for your course	Wilcoxon signed rank test	Use Wilcoxon signed rank test
Independent groups	Chi-squared	Mann–Whitney U-test	Use Mann–Whitney U-test
Correlation **Ordinal data (or interval data)**			
Spearman			

Table 47 Which test to use?

You can work out from the table what test to use in the different situations, such as that the test for a test of difference, nominal data, independent groups, is the Chi-squared test.

Doing the statistical test

Your examination papers will have the formulae for the statistical tests in the front so you can use them if asked to carry out calculations. You should take a calculator into the examination. Practise doing the tests using made up figures — you will find that it is not as hard as it might look at first. You will have done statistical testing for your practical investigation, which will help. Follow step-by-step instructions to unpick the formula for each test and practise.

A-level students, make sure that you can choose a test for a study, and that you can give reasons for your choice. Learn the brief summary given here as it has the information that you need. It is probably worth learning the information off by heart if you find it hard to work out.

What test is needed for a test of difference if the design is repeated measures and the data are at least ordinal?

Content Guidance

Choosing a level of significance

You have to test how far results are likely to be due to chance. Three **levels of significance** are summarised here to show what a level of significance is. Use your textbook or another source to make sure you understand fully what p≤.05 stands for (or .01 or .10).

- 0.10 is 10% being due to chance — not acceptable
- 0.05 is 5% being due to chance — acceptable
- 0.01 is 1% being due to chance — better and more acceptable

> **Exam tip**
>
> It is worth spending a little time learning this section about levels of significance. Although it might seem complicated if it is the first time you have come across the idea, it is less complicated the more you read it — don't let the numbers and apparent level of complication put you off.

Levels of measurement

For your course in psychology, there are three **levels of measurement**:

- **nominal** = data in categories
- **ordinal** = data that are ranked
- **interval/ratio** = data that are mathematical measurements

If you are doing the AS course you do not need to know about levels of measurement for the exam.

Null hypothesis

The hypothesis is the statement of what is expected to happen in a study (page 46), and the **null hypothesis** states that it will not happen, because any difference or relationship will be due to chance. It is the null hypothesis that is tested by an inferential test because the test determines how far the results are due to chance rather than what was expected, and whether what was expected has happened or not. Use your textbook or some other source to see how to write out a null hypothesis.

> **Exam tip**
>
> When writing the alternate or experimental hypothesis (or null) make sure that both the independent variable (IV) and the dependent variable (DV) are fully explained (operationalised). For example, if the IV is whether someone is driving a large or small car, say so and do not just say 'the car they drive'.

One-tailed or two-tailed

A hypothesis is directional if it says which way the results will go. In testing, directional is called '**one-tailed**'.

A hypothesis is non-directional if it does not specify which way the result will go. In testing, non-directional is called '**two-tailed**'.

> **Exam tip**
>
> Note that these levels of measurement, along with experimental design (independent groups, matched pairs, repeated measures or correlation) are needed for choosing an inferential test. Though it may seem that there is a lot to learn in the area of inferential testing, it is worth rereading the sections as it is less than you may think.

> **Knowledge check 30**
>
> If you collect data from a questionnaire about people's memory for events and ask whether people have a good or a bad memory for events, what level of measurement are the data you have collected?

> **Knowledge check 31**
>
> Write out the null hypothesis for a study that suggests that older people (60+ years old) would remember fewer words from a list of 30 words than younger people (20 to 30 years old) would.

Critical and observed values

The result of doing an inferential test is the **observed value**. For each type of inferential test there are tables of **critical values**, against which you can check your observed value to see if your result is significant.

AS students will not need to use critical values tables in the examination.

How to compare critical and observed values

- First you need to know your observed value, from working out the test result. In your practical investigation in cognitive psychology you will have carried out either a Wilcoxon or a Mann–Whitney U-test, which will have given you a result U or T. For the biological approach you will have worked out the result of a Spearman, giving you a *rho* value. For the learning approach you will have worked out the result of a Chi-squared test, giving you the Chi-squared value (χ^2).
- Then you need the right critical values table. These tables are found in statistics books or on the internet (and in your examination papers as well as at the back of your specification). Find the right table for each test.
- Then you need to know: for the Spearman test and the Wilcoxon test, the number of participants; for the Mann–Whitney U-test, the number of participants in each group (this will have been an independent groups design); for the Chi-squared test, the degrees of freedom, which for a 2 by 2 table is 1.
- Finally, choose a level of significance of 0.05 (5%) and decide whether your hypothesis is one- or two-tailed.
- Using this information, look along the rows and columns of the table and compare your observed value with the critical value to see if the result is significant or not.
- The table will tell you whether your result has to be equal to, larger or smaller than the one in the appropriate box of the table and you get this information in the front of each examination paper too.

Type I and Type II errors

It is possible that accepting the alternate or experimental hypothesis and rejecting the null hypothesis was not correct, and this could be seen if other studies were to be done, with different findings. If a researcher has over-optimistically accepted the alternate/experimental hypothesis (saying the study worked), this is called a Type I error and if they have pessimistically accepted the null hypothesis (saying the study did not work) this is a Type II error.

Case studies of brain-damaged patients, including HM

Henry Molaison (HM) is a well-known participant whose memory was widely studied for a great many years. Case studies gather both qualitative data and quantitative data. Case studies are in depth and detailed, focusing on often one participant or a small group of participants.

- Schmolck et al. (2002) included material from work with HM in their case study as well as other patients. They found that the lateral temporal cortex was important for semantic knowledge (semantic = meaning) and the more damage there was the more impairment.
- Phineas Gage (1823–60) is someone who had damage to the prefrontal lobe following an accident. His behaviour seemed to become more unrestrained after

Exam tip

Make up some results for either a Mann–Whitney U or a Wilcoxon test and see if your results are significant given fictitious levels of significance, number of participants and other features.

Exam tip

In the sample answer materials (SAMs) that are on the Edexcel website there are some questions asking about statistics and significance (e.g. A-level Paper 2) to give you an idea about questions that might be asked.

Knowledge check 32

For the Mann–Whitney U-test you need to know the number of participants in each group, whereas for the Wilcoxon test you need just the number of participants. Explain this point.

Exam tip

Remember that Type I (One) starts with an 'O' so that is being 'Optimistic', whereas a Type II error is more negative.

the accident suggesting that the prefrontal lobe is for problem solving and decision making, which bring restraint to people's behaviour.

■ Henry Molaison had surgery for epilepsy when he was 26 in 1953 and the result was amnesia, hence the conclusion that damage to the brain in certain regions causes memory difficulties and so 'memory' of some sort must take place in those regions. The damage was related to the medial temporal lobe and therein lies the hippocampus among other brain areas, and it is generally thought from case studies of those with brain damage that these are relevant areas for memory.

Strengths	Weaknesses
When there is more than one case study available showing the same brain damage (more or less) with the same difficulties in cognitive functioning, one set of results backs the other and there is reliability in the findings	There are many variables involved in cognitive processing including a lot of brain regions. It is hard to pick out one structure that is for one aspect of memory and processing
Measurements from brain scanning using images produced can be tested for reliability as other people can make the measurements to check them	Neuroimaging might be good for large damage but small sites of damage might not be picked up by scanning
There is scientific credibility because of careful study of the brain damage and controlled experiments to look at cognitive processing	Damage to the brain rarely occurs just in one specific area without damaging surrounding areas and those surrounding areas might be where the relevant processing might take place

Table 48 Strengths and weaknesses of using case studies of patients with brain damage in research

Summary

■ There are two types of experiment (in your course): field and laboratory.
■ Experiments have an independent variable and a dependent variable, which must both be carefully operationalised (they need to be made measurable).
■ An experimental hypothesis is a statement of what is expected and can be directional or non-directional. The null hypothesis states that the hypothesis is 'not the case' (e.g 'more words will not be recalled if...').
■ There are three experimental designs: repeated measures, independent groups and matched pairs.
■ Experiments have careful controls to rule out participant and situational variables as well as experimenter effects and demand

characteristics. Controlling for extraneous variables can mean no confounding variables.
■ Bias is more contained if there are no order effects and if conditions are either counterbalanced or randomised.
■ Results are displayed using measures of central tendency (averages), measures of dispersion (e.g. range) and graphs (including bar graphs, histograms and frequency graphs).
■ Results are tested using inferential statistical tests.
■ Issues around claiming that results are secure include objectivity (subjectivity and interpretation bring bias), validity (findings must relate to real life) and reliability (a study has to be shown to get the same results no matter how often the study is done).
■ Validity includes internal, predictive and ecological validity.

Studies

You need to know about the classic study and one of three contemporary studies. The contemporary studies include Schmolck et al. (2002) or Steyvers and Hemmer (2012), but it is Sebastián and Hernández-Gil (2012) that is used in this book. You may prefer to revise one of the other two if you studied one of them.

Classic study: Baddeley (1966b)

The classic study here links to the models of memory and helps to illustrate those models, including the multi-store model and the idea of episodic and semantic memory. Baddeley (1966b) focused on memory for sound and memory for meaning. Short-term memory is supposed to be using sound so acoustic similarity in a list of words would pose more difficulty than semantic similarity. Baddeley (1966b) wanted to see if the same would be true in long-term memory. Use your textbook or another source to recall the procedure of Baddeley (1966b).

Results

Experiment 1

The order of the words was not so well recalled in the acoustically similar list in Experiment 1, but there was not so much forgetting in that list either — according to the recall after the break, following the initial recall. In the semantically similar list, the recall was not different from that in the control list. It was the acoustic similarity that caused difficulties.

However, recall involved both STM (the immediate recall of the list of words) and LTM (the later recall and the re-test). So Baddeley could not draw conclusions about LTM as he wanted to.

Experiment 2

When there was interference to stop recall using what was in STM there was an effect. This showed that Experiment 1 findings did not give Baddeley the results he needed. He needed to use interference to block STM, to test LTM properly.

Experiment 3

Interference was used to block STM. Recall in the 'acoustically similar' condition and the control condition was very similar, including at re-test. In LTM acoustic similarity did not affect the recall of the order of the words. In the semantically similar list recall was much better in the control condition. The semantic similarity affected recall in LTM.

Conclusion

It was found that long-term memory is affected by semantic similarity but not by acoustic similarity. This is different from what is found in short-term memory, where acoustic similarity is more problematic. The results showed that in LTM learning was affected by the meaning of words more than if the words sounded alike. This is evidence that LTM uses semantic coding (which compares with evidence from other studies that STM uses acoustic coding). Baddeley (1966b) showed that coding in STM is different from coding in LTM.

Evaluation

Strengths	Weaknesses
Baddeley's (1966b) study used careful controls and an experimental design, such as controlling for the time a stimulus was available for. This means the study can show cause-and-effect conclusions because of controls over extraneous variables	The study can be said to lack ecological validity as Baddeley used lists of words and adjectives to test coding of STM and LTM and these are not naturalistic tasks. Steyvers and Hemmer (2012) explain how when they used pictures of scenes to look at reconstructive memory they had different results from other studies that had not had such realism
The study used different conditions and three experiments as part of the main study, with the result that within the main study Baddeley (1966b) had replications and could claim reliability. Reliability is required if a study is to add to a body of knowledge	The study reduces memory to how well the order of lists of 10 words is recalled when lists have certain conditions (e.g. the list of words being acoustically similar). This links to the weakness of the study not having valid findings. Reductionism can help with reliability and experimental findings but lacks a holistic look at something, so may not study everyday life

Table 49 Strengths and weaknesses of Baddeley (1966b)

Questions & Answers

Cognitive psychology Studies Q1 and Q2 are on Baddeley's (1996b) study.

Contemporary study: Sebastián and Hernández-Gil (2012)

Sebastián and Hernández-Gil (2012) looked at memory span in Spanish young people of different ages and older people too, to see how memory span develops through the lifespan. Use a textbook or other source to remind yourself of the aims and procedure of their study.

Results

The first part showed that the 5 year olds had a very low digit span (3.76), much lower than the other age groups. From 6 to 8 years there was a similar digit span (4.34), higher than for the 5 year olds. The increase from 4 to 5 digits as the span occurred at 9 years old and rose to 11 years old (5.13). The 12 to 14 year olds again matched one another, but differed from others older than them. The 15 to 17 years showed a similar digit span (5.83).

The second part used data from their 2010 study. It found that those with Alzheimer's dementia had a digit span of 4.20, those with fronto-temporal dementia had a digit span of 4.22 and those who were healthy older people (the controls) had a span of 4.44.

Healthy older people had a higher digit span than 5 year olds and 6 year olds but did not differ from the other groups. Those with Alzheimer's dementia had a higher span than 5 year olds but did not differ from the other groups. Those with the other type of dementia had a similar span to the youngest groups.

Conclusions

- Digit span increases from 5 to 17 years.
- The English data (data from English speakers) had digit span increasing to 15 years old and then not after that, whereas, the Spanish study found an increase up to 17 years old. The English data showed an adult span of about 7 digits. The Spanish data showed a lower digit span (about 1 digit below), which the researchers thought

Exam tip

Be sure to learn enough about the different parts of a study (aims, procedure, results, conclusions, evaluation) so that you can answer a question about one of these parts as well as a question about the whole study.

Knowledge check 33

Explain the four lists that Baddeley (1966b) used.

Exam tip

Learn actual figures when preparing information for a question about a study, where there are figures, as there are here. Including figures adds detail to the information you give and explains the results much more fully.

was down to the length of a Spanish 'number' word, longer than English words for numbers. This can link to the idea of subvocal rehearsal that fits Baddeley's working memory model.

- Older healthy people have a digit span matching that of a 7 year old, showing a decline from adult digit span over time.
- Those with dementia had a lower digit span, matching those of 6 year olds, but not that much different from that of healthy older people so dementia does not seem to affect digit span, though age does.

Evaluation

Strengths	Weaknesses
There is reliability as the study uses data from other studies and finds a very similar set of results	Validity might be weak as this is an artificial task. However, the task is there to test the phonological loop so the task might be valid in that sense
Cause-and-effect conclusions, that digit span increases with age, can be drawn reasonably well because of the good and careful controls	The study states the digit span and shows this increases with age but it is more descriptive than explanatory perhaps when it comes to when subvocal rehearsal starts and how it is used

Table 50 Strengths and weaknesses of Sebastián and Hernández-Gil (2012)

Summary

- Baddeley (1966b) is the classic study in cognitive psychology in your course. His aim was to look at the mode of representation for long-term memory, leading on from the idea that short-term memory uses acoustic processing.
- Baddeley found that short-term memory did use acoustic processing but long-term memory relied on semantic processing, so was different from short-term memory.
- Sebastián and Hernández-Gill (2012) is one contemporary study in cognitive psychology in

your course. The researchers looked at digit span and its length depending on age.
- They found that the youngest children had the smallest digit span and as children get older they have a longer digit span up to about 17 years old, when it levels off to an adult level.
- They found that older people have a reasonably short digit span but that having dementia does not affect the digit span.

> **Knowledge check 34**
>
> What were three aims of Sebastián and Hernández-Gil (2012)?

Key question

How can psychologists' understanding of memory help patients with dementia?

Describing the key question

The number of people with dementia is increasing, for example, according to the Alzheimer's society 800,000 people have dementia in the UK, set to rise to 1 million by 2021. This is clearly something of relevance to society. Dementia refers to problems in the brain that cause information-processing difficulties, including memory problems and problems with functioning. The key question is how psychological understanding has been able to help those with dementia.

Application of concepts and ideas

- Although dementia is about memory loss, it is not that people with dementia lose all their memory. Episodic memory can be affected. It can be helpful to understand that someone with dementia might 'live in the past' and to be with that person at that time in their past (i.e. go with their memories and do not contradict them).
- Short-term memory can be affected. A way to help would be to be very specific when asking questions rather than asking more general questions, to try to cue memories if possible. For example, rather than asking 'have you had visitors today?' ask 'has Jean, your daughter, been to visit you today?'
- Working memory theory has suggested that different tasks done at the same time using the same type of processing can be very difficult. If someone with dementia is trying to attend to what someone is saying they will do so better without background noise, for example.
- If memories are reconstructed using prior experiences and schemas, then someone with dementia who seems to be saying something that does not make sense might be using mixed schemas and muddled episodic memories so listen carefully and ask limited questions, but try to follow the thought processes of the individual.

Questions & Answers

Cognitive psychology Key question Q1 focuses on this key question.

Summary

- Learning more about dementia can help to devise ways to help people with dementia.
- Dementia is a growing issue in the UK and is expensive for society so is a key and contemporary issue.
- Knowing about short-term memory can help. Giving someone time to rehearse information and asking specific questions can limit what has to be encoded.
- Working memory ideas suggest it is hard to process information using the same 'channels' so if someone with dementia is processing sound keep other sound to a minimum.
- Reconstructive memory ideas show that we use schemas and past knowledge when remembering, so cues to prompt past understanding can help.
- Another key issue that cognitive psychology can help with is learning techniques such as revision. The multi-store model of memory, for example, suggests rehearsal is required so that knowledge goes into long-term memory, so it is known that giving rehearsal time is necessary.

Practical investigation

You will have carried out at least one practical within cognitive psychology, which will have been an experiment. Go back over your notes to revise what you did, as it is not possible here to help you to revise that part of the course.

Some general ideas about the practical and what to learn

Make sure you know about:
- the aim(s) and purpose(s) of the practical
- your experimental hypothesis and null hypothesis and whether directional or not

- the independent and dependent variable (fully operationalised)
- the participant design and why you chose it
- the sampling method, why you chose it, and what other method you might have chosen
- ethical issues and how they were or should have been dealt with
- the apparatus and why you chose it
- what you did about order effects (if you used repeated measures)
- what controls you put into place and why — and what was not controlled
- two problems with your study, apart from ethical issues and controls
- possible issues with regard to experimenter effects
- strengths of your study — considering issues such as validity, reliability, generalisability, objectivity/subjectivity and credibility
- which descriptive statistics you used (mean, median, mode, range, graphs) and why
- how to draw and interpret a frequency graph
- which statistical test you used, why, and with what result, including the chosen level of significance
- how to write up the procedure, results and discussion sections of a report

Exam tip

To revise your practical, focus on issues like experimental design, controls, ethics, how you manipulated the IV and how you measured the DV. Be ready to evaluate your study as well. One way of preparing might be to explain to someone else the whole practical, including evaluation points.

Knowledge check 36

What was your IV, your DV, one control and one way you solved an ethical issue?

Questions & Answers

Cognitive psychology Practical Q1 gives answers focusing on your practical.

Summary

- The practical has to be a laboratory experiment and has to include aspects covered in the material specified for cognitive psychology.
- Ethical principles must be followed.
- Research design decisions are important in experiments (as in other research methods), such as the experimental design itself, decisions of how to control participant and situational variables, decisions about manipulation of the IV and decisions about how to measure the DV.
- The results must be analysed using measures of central tendency (mean, median and mode, as appropriate) and dispersion (range and standard deviation).
- Bar charts, histograms and frequency graphs are on the specification.
- Use the right statistical test (from Mann–Whitney U and Wilcoxon) and know about how you used it, the results and so on.
- The data are to be commented on as well, which can include evaluation of your study.

Issues and debates (A-level only)

If you are studying for the AS, you do not need to know about issues and debates.

For the A-level there is a topic at the end of your course, Topic 9, which has 'issues and debates' as a section. To help A-level students become familiar with the 11 'issues and debates' ready for this Topic 9 section, they are explained at the end of each topic area. In cognitive psychology the 11 issues and debates are listed in the specification and material from cognitive psychology is used to illustrate each issue and debate.

Content Guidance

Issues and debates in psychology	Links to cognitive psychology in your course
Ethical issues in research	Case studies such as HM raise difficult ethical issues around confidentiality and getting informed consent, as well as giving the right to withdraw. These issues are about respect, competence, responsibility and integrity.
Practical issues in research	The validity of experiments is an issue that is difficult to overcome as are issues around controlling all variables that might be confounding variables.
Reductionism	The memory models break memory up into different aspects of information processing, which is reductionist in approach and might miss understanding that a more holistic approach might uncover.
Explaining using different themes	The different models of memory use different themes.
Psychology as a science	Cognitive psychology uses a scientific approach to studying how we process information, such as experiments and controls (e.g. Baddeley 1966b).
Cultural and gender issues in research	Sebastián and Hernández-Gil (2012) compare Spanish speakers with English speakers and suggest digit span is different because of length of words — not really cultural differences but might have been interpreted as such.
Nature-nurture	Reconstructive memory ideas emphasise that our experiences have a role in remembering, so our development might affect our recall, in giving us certain experiences.
Development over time	The multi-store model started off the STM/LTM split that is still studied. Though scanning and different research methods have enabled a more rigorous study of the brain and of its processing. Baddeley has been working on short-term and long-term memory from the 1960s to well into the twenty-first century. His work is now being used to help those with dementia. Sebastián and Hernández (2012) looked at digit span, finding in adults 7+/−2 was about right, as Miller found in the 1950s.
Social control	Understanding about reconstructive memory might mean in some situations, such as in court, there might be manipulation (e.g. using leading questions).
Use of psychology within society	The key question shows how psychology is used within society.
Socially sensitive research	Memory loss, such as from dementia, is a sensitive area and studying such issues can need careful attention to ethics, as well as using psychology in such areas.

Table 51 Issues and debates and how cognitive psychology illustrates each

Questions & Answers

Cognitive psychology Issues and debates Q1 focuses on practical issues in the design of studies both in social and cognitive psychology.

Exam tip

The 11 issues and debates are repeated at the end of each topic area to show how that topic area illustrates them. You could make notes for each issue and debate, drawing together all the ideas in the topic areas, so that you have a wide range of examples of that issue/debate.

Summary: cognitive psychology

After studying this topic area, you should be able to understand, apply and evaluate:

- the working memory model
- the multi-store model
- episodic and semantic memory
- reconstructive memory
- using experiments in psychology and related issues
- analysis of quantitative data, non-inferential
- analysis of quantitative data using inferential statistical testing
- use of case studies of brain-damaged patients including HM, and issues of qualitative data

- Baddeley (1966b) as the classic study and Sebastián and Hernández-Gil (2012) as the chosen contemporary study (you may wish to revise a different contemporary study)
- one key question relating to the material in cognitive psychology in your course
- one practical investigation that you will have done while studying this topic area
- if you are studying A-level, issues and debates reflected in cognitive psychology in your course

Questions & Answers

This section follows the structure of the course, with social psychology first and then cognitive psychology. The questions follow the course structure within each area too:

- overview of the topic
- content
- method
- studies
- key question
- practical
- issues and debates (illustrated in cognitive psychology only — A-level only)

Unless otherwise stated, the example questions can be used as practice questions for both AS and A-level Paper 1 — and for the methods sections and the issues and debates section, A-level Paper 3 too, as indicated.

The difference between the AS and A-level papers is that there will be more marks awarded for AO1 at AS. There will also be no issues and debates at AS.

Examination issues

Assessment objectives

You are marked according to assessment objectives (AOs). You can find these in the specification, but they are summarised here:

- **AO1** — knowledge with understanding of scientific ideas, processes, techniques and procedures (knowing and understanding)
- **AO2** — applying knowledge and understanding of scientific ideas, processes, techniques and procedures (applying)
- **AO3** — analysing, interpreting and evaluating a range of scientific information, ideas and evidence to make judgements and reach conclusions and also to refine practical design and procedures (commenting)

A good plan is to consider the exam paper as covering the three AOs in equal proportions (one third each) and to consider the four topic areas and sections within them to be covered evenly. That will help you when preparing.

Exam questions and marking

For both AS and A-level, your exams will have some points-based marking and some levels-based marking:

- up to 8 marks is likely to mean points based, which means 1 mark for each point clearly made
- 8 marks and over is likely to be levels marking, which means a mark depending on where in bands the answer fits

AS Papers 1 and 2: expect short-answer questions that are points-based and some extended writing, some with 8 marks and one with 12 marks (though not focusing on issues and debates).

A-level Paper 1: expect short-answer questions that are points-based. Also some 8-mark questions and at the end a 12-mark question on issues and debates.

A-level Paper 3: some of the short-answer method questions can suit A-level Paper 3, as can some of the questions on studies and issues and debates. Where a question in this guide suits Paper 3 that is noted.

Extended open-response questions: allocation of AOs

The different mark allocations for extended open-response questions have different assessment objective splits. Extended open-response questions are from 8 marks onwards:

- 8 marks can be split into: AO1 4 marks and AO2* 4 marks; or AO1 4 marks and AO3 4 marks
- 12 marks can be split into: AO1 4 marks, AO2* 4 marks and AO3 4 marks; or AO1 6 marks, AO3 6 marks
- 16 marks can be split into: AO1 6 marks, AO2* 4 marks and AO3 6 marks; or AO1 6 marks and AO3 10 marks
- 20 marks can be split into: AO1 8 marks, AO2* 4 marks and AO3 8 marks; or AO1 8 marks and AO3 12 marks

*You will know if you need to focus on AO2 (applying your knowledge and understanding) because there will be a scenario of some sort to apply it to and a comment about you needing to refer to the scenario. Without a scenario to apply your knowledge and understanding to, the marks will be AO1 and AO3 with the splits as outlined here.

Exam advice

All questions and answers are followed by exam advice. These are preceded by the icon ⓔ or ⓔ. They indicate what a question requires, where credit is due, strengths in the answer, areas for improvement, specific problems, common errors, lack of clarity, irrelevance, mistakes in the meaning of terms and/or misinterpretation of the question. The comments also indicate how the answers might be marked in an exam — there are ticks in the answers to show where exactly marks are awarded. Note that where there is more than one answer, the Student A answer is the strongest.

■ Social psychology

Overview

(1) Describe what is meant by social psychology. (4 marks)

ⓔ This question tests AO1, knowledge and understanding. Think about any assumptions underlying the approach. It would be useful to give an example to show understanding, but the example must be fully explained, not just mentioned. This question would be marked on a point-by-point basis so you are looking for four brief points or two well-elaborated points.

> **Student answer**
>
> Social psychology looks at people as groups and how they behave in groups. ✓ For example, social identity theory suggests that self-esteem is to do with identifying with a group, and this means in-group favouritism and out-group hostility, which explains prejudice. ✓ Social psychology looks at people as social beings, including issues such as why some individuals obey others even when it goes against their own moral code. Social psychology focuses on an individual, but more on how an individual fits in with others within a society than on the individual themselves. ✓ There is a focus on interactions between people; issues such as crowd behaviour, helping others, prejudice and obedience are examples of topics covered. ✓

ⓔ **4/4 marks awarded.** This answer relies on examples quite a lot, but that is fine because they are clearly explained to show the underlying principles of the approach, such as the focus on groups and interactions between individuals. If you are using an example, make sure you either give quite a few instances, as in the last point, or you explain fully, as in the second point.

Content

(1) What is meant by the term 'obedience'? (2 marks)

ⓔ This is 'points based', 1 mark for each point, knowledge with understanding (AO1). Give a definition of obedience. A simple definition will gain 1 mark and a more detailed definition will gain the 2 marks.

> **Student answer**
>
> Obedience is when people obey others in authority. ✓

ⓔ **1/2 marks awarded.** It is not sufficient to say that obedience is when people obey (0 marks), but saying that they obey others in authority is enough for 1 mark. For full marks, this would need more detail, such as mentioning that obeying means you are in an agentic state, or saying that someone is acting on orders even if doing that goes against their moral code so they experience moral strain. It is good to give an example, such as when someone moves a car because a parking attendant tells them to.

(2) Describe Milgram's agency theory of obedience. (4 marks)

(e) There are 4 marks here (points based), all for describing what is meant by the agency theory (AO1). Including an example is a good idea as it helps to illustrate your answer and show that you understand the theory, but keep it short as it is worth no more than 1 mark.

Student answer

In Milgram's study, the participants denied to themselves that they were responsible for their actions. They allowed the experimenter to take responsibility for what was happening. When you are not acting under your own control but because of the orders of someone else, you are their agent, and this is called being in an agentic state. ✓✓

(e) **2/4 marks awarded.** The 2 marks are awarded here for saying what an agentic state is, although the answer is not well focused on the question. The other 2 marks could be gained by linking this to Milgram's study and showing that the participants said they felt they had to continue and were just obeying orders. This was his agency theory of obedience — that people were not making their own decisions. The answer could have said that the opposite of the agentic state is being autonomous and acting on one's own decisions, whereas being in an agentic state means doing what someone in authority says, which is probably necessary in order for society to function.

(3) Evaluate social identity theory as an explanation of prejudice. (4 marks)

(e) Note that for short 'evaluate' questions you do not have to describe at all. Assume that the examiner knows what the theory is. All 4 marks (points based) are for evaluation (AO3). You could say that another theory explains prejudice better or contradicts this one, or you could criticise the research methods used to arrive at the theory (perhaps researchers used laboratory experiments that are not valid). If you mention an alternative theory there is likely to be only 1 mark, because if you then start looking more at that alternative theory you are addressing a different question. 'Evaluate' questions require a judgement at the end of the answer.

Student answer

Many studies have shown that we prefer our in-group and are less interested in any out-group, and their findings are evidence for the theory. Tajfel did a lot of work in this area, and others have too. It seems that we boost our self-esteem by siding with an in-group, which means going against an out-group. So social identity theory (SIT) seems a reasonable explanation and we have evidence for it. ✓ It can also explain the findings of other studies of prejudice, even if they are said to be about another theory. For example, Minard carried out a study of miners. The study could be explained by saying that the miners were an in-group when working, but when above ground, they were no longer an in-group (not being 'miners' any more but going home to different roles). ✓ Also Sherif's study at Robber's Cave, although arriving at the theory of realistic conflict as an explanation of prejudice, did look at in-group and out-group behaviour between the Rattlers and Eagles and found out-group hostility, as social identity theory predicts. ✓ However, much of the research was done using experiments and falsely formed groups, so the conclusions might not be valid and might not represent real-life behaviour. ✓

ⓔ **4/4 marks awarded.** 1 mark is awarded for saying that there is a lot of evidence (although this needs elaboration, as is done here, by giving Tajfel). A further mark is given for the Minard example and showing how SIT can explain it. Minard is probably a new study for you and shows that it is useful to go beyond your textbook. You could add more about evidence instead (e.g. experiments are reliable) to get the mark. Another mark is for the reference to the theory being useful in explaining Sherif's findings. The final mark is for the methodological criticism of the lack of validity.

Method (also A-level Paper 3)

(1) **Give *one* strength and *one* weakness of questionnaires as a research method.** (4 marks)

ⓔ There are 2 marks for the strength and 2 marks for the weakness — they are points based and for AO3 evaluation. Do not just give a brief answer for each — be sure to expand your answer enough for the full 2 marks. For example, say what the strength is, and then say something else to explain it further or give an example. Make your answer specific to questionnaires not just any method.

> **Student answer**
>
> One strength is that a lot of people can be reached relatively cheaply by posting questionnaires or by handing them out in busy areas. Compared with an experiment, many participants can be reached and potentially can contribute data. More people can mean more generalisability. ✓✓ A weakness is that there can be a poor response rate. When a lot of people are asked, it is likely that many will not post the questionnaire back, or that people will refuse to complete it if asked personally. A poor response rate can mean a biased sample (a volunteer sample) and bias in replies ✓✓

ⓔ **4/4 marks awarded.** A strength and a weakness are correctly identified, for 1 mark each, and there is some expansion in each case, so full marks.

(2) **An interview using a set list of questions was carried out with 20 people who happened to be in a town on a Tuesday afternoon and agreed to take part. The aim was to find out whether people preferred those who were like them or were happier meeting and finding out about people who were different.**

(a) **What type of interview was being used?** (1 mark)

ⓔ This is worth 1 AO2 mark (applying your understanding). You have studied three types of interview and you need to choose the one that fits this stimulus material.

> **Student answer**
>
> Structured interview. ✓

ⓔ 1/1 mark awarded. This is the right answer — there is a set list of questions.

(b) What sampling was used? Explain your answer. (2 marks)

ⓔ There are 2 marks available, one for the sampling type (if justified) and one for the justification (AO2). You have studied four sampling types, and two of these will fit the stimulus material, so choose one and explain this choice for the second mark.

Student answer A

This is volunteer sampling. ✓ Only those who stopped and agreed would have completed the interview, and this would mean the participants had volunteered and were self-selecting. ✓

ⓔ 2/2 marks awarded. This is right and the justification is clear, so both marks are given.

Student answer B

Opportunity sampling. ✓

ⓔ 1/2 marks awarded. This is a right answer but it needs explaining — that only those in that town on a Tuesday afternoon are going to be in the sample. There could be 1 mark for saying 'opportunity', but it is also possible that this mark will only be given if it is clear that this knowledge is accompanied by understanding (you need to show you know what opportunity sampling is). Try to do more than just name the sampling method.

(c) Give two possible problems with the sampling method used. (2 marks)

ⓔ There is 1 mark for each problem (AO3), and 'give' does not mean you have to say anything about the problems. However, the problems need to be clear enough to be understood. The problems can be general issues concerning the sampling method, as the question does not say you have to relate to the stimulus material.

Student answer

Volunteer sampling means only those willing to take part do so; in this case, those with time will be in the sample, which means there is bias. ✓ Another related problem is that volunteers might be those of a certain gender, perhaps the same gender as the person carrying out the interviews, which again might mean bias. ✓

ⓔ 2/2 marks awarded. There are 2 marks here, 1 for the factor of 'having time' and the other for 'gender'. The possible problems are clearly given.

(d) Explain two advantages of using the type of interview used. (4 marks)

ⓔ There are 2 marks (AO3) for each advantage and nothing for disadvantages. To 'explain' the advantage you need to be clear about why it is good and how it relates to the type of interview, which in this case is structured interviewing.

Student answer

One advantage is the ease of analysis, because structured interviews ask all participants the same questions and the answers, therefore, can be confidently compared. ✓ Another advantage is that anyone can carry out the interview, because the questions are clearly listed and there is no deviation from them, ✓ so interviewers do not have to be trained in how to explore issues as they would be for an unstructured interview, and this saves time and cost for researchers. ✓

ⓔ **3/4 marks awarded.** Only 3 marks are gained as there is not enough elaboration on the first advantage. The second advantage explains that, because there is no deviation from the questions, anyone can carry out the interviews, and then there is elaboration saying that this reduces the need for using only trained interviewers. The explanation of the first advantage, however, while noting that having the same questions means answers can be compared, does not elaborate on how this can be done or why this is useful. An elaboration could be that there is no problem with trying to compare the answers, unlike unstructured interviews, in which questions are explored further and differently for each respondent.

(e) **Explain one factor that might make the findings of this research lack validity.** (2 marks)

ⓔ The question asks about validity (AO3), which refers to how 'real-life' the results of the source study will be. Consider one feature that would mean the results might be artificial, and make sure you say why this would be the case, so that you get the 2 marks. Consider this particular structured interview (such as the specific situation).

Student answer

The participants are in their natural situation, being in town on that Tuesday afternoon, but being asked about their feelings about 'meeting someone new' — which the interviewer is — so that might affect their replies. ✓ This might be because of demand characteristics as they think that the answer is 'I like meeting someone new', or it might be down to social desirability, as they think it is polite to say they 'like meeting someone new'. Either would give bias. ✓ Also they might not be thinking about such things and might just say anything to get away.

ⓔ **2/2 marks awarded.** This answer is thorough and gets both marks. The factor is identified as 'being affected by being asked the questions' and the answer then explains this more fully by saying that there might be demand characteristics (explained) or social desirability (explained). The comment about wanting to get away is really a different factor so does not link to the question. You can see that even though there are only 2 marks, the answer has to be reasonably thorough to make sure the points are clear. Using terms is good.

(f) **Given what you know about social identity, what would you expect to find from the interview? Explain your answer.** (2 marks)

ⓔ There are 2 marks available here for applying theory to a source (AO2). You do not have to explain social identity theory, but you could summarise it briefly and then link to the aim of the interview and what results would be expected.

Social identity theory suggests that self-esteem comes from being in a group with others and identifying with that group — which is then treated as better than an out-group so that self-esteem is good. So it would be expected that people prefer people from their in-group, operationalised as being 'like them', rather than people from the out-group, operationalised as people who are 'different'. ✓✓

e **2/2 marks awarded.** This answer gets both marks because the link to social identity theory is clear and the question is answered clearly too — people are more likely to like people in their in-group than those in their out-group.

Studies

(1) **Describe the results and conclusions of Burger (2009), Corhs et al. (2012) or Reicher and Haslam (2006).** (5 marks)

e This questions is worth 5 AO1 marks, which are points based. It focuses on the results and conclusions, not on the aims or procedure of the studies so do not describe these. As you need both results *and* conclusions, it is unlikely that you would get full marks if you do not address both. You can answer this question using one of the other contemporary studies if you are not revising Burger (2009). Make sure you include enough details to gain 5 marks. It should be clear which study you are using.

Student answer

Burger (2009) found that 70% in the main condition went to carry on after 150 volts compared with 82.5% in Experiment 5 (Milgram, 1974) and this was comparable. ✓ Also in Burger's study 63.3% went to carry on in the modelled refusal condition, not statistically different from the base condition (70%), even though a difference was expected. ✓ There were no real gender differences in obedience in Burger's study, though women seemed more reluctant to continue in the condition where another teacher refused. Again similar to Milgram's findings. ✓ In conclusion, Burger (2009) felt that the answer to whether the same level of obedience that Milgram found in 1960/1970 was found in 2009 — obedience was the same or very similar .The same situational factors seem to be around today as in the time of Milgram's work. ✓ Even with Burger's changes, obedience was similarly high as in Milgram's studies. Gender did not seem to have an effect and having another teacher refuse did not have much of an effect on obedience, so Burger concluded that obedience was down to the situation, as Milgram thought. ✓

e **5/5 marks awarded.** This answer works through the results and conclusions in order and is clear and detailed. Each point that gets a mark is expressed clearly. There are comments comparing Burger's findings with Milgram's — although these are not really needed as no evaluation is asked for. By comparing the findings the results and conclusions are being explained as Burger's aim was to compare with Milgram so his conclusions needed to be about that. So the answer has good depth and detail.

(2) Assess the generalisability of Sherif et al. (1954/1961).   (3 marks)

(Also A-level Paper 3)

ⓔ This questions is worth 3 AO3 marks, which are points based. Be sure to write enough for 3 marks and only evaluate using generalisability, not other issues. You are trying to say three things, although it is possible to gain more than 1 mark for a good, well-made point. Generalisability is about the sample, so discuss the sample in your answer and its limitations and/or strengths. End with a conclusion.

> **Student answer**
>
> Sherif et al. used boys at a summer camp. They were around 11 years old so it would not be possible to generalise to others apart from 11 year old boys. ✓ They were matched by teachers in terms of issues like IQ as well as screened with regard to home background, so that helped with comparing how the two groups behaved, but it restricted the range of the sample (for example, those with issues in their home background were not chosen, and so limits generalisability to boys in the same categories). ✓

ⓔ **2/3 marks awarded.** The first mark shows understanding of what generalisability is, which is helpful, and gives clear information about the sample. The second mark is for talking about the matching and how that would limit the sample as those not in those categories would not get into the sample. This is a good point. However, there is not enough for another mark. The answer could talk about the culture of the boys (in the USA, all from Oklahoma, from Protestant families, which is limiting the generalisability, for example). Note how much detail is required for a question like this — more than is in this guide — so be sure to learn enough about studies.

Key question

(1) Discuss the issues in the source below, using concepts from the social approach.   (8 marks)

> Fighting broke out between two local villages when a visiting rugby team from one of the villages won an annual competition by 28 points. At first, the fight was only between two of the players who had clashed during the match, but soon the fighting spread and police had to be called. Elders from one of the villages explained that there had been prejudice between the two villages for years, ever since a factory was built near one village. This had brought good road links and jobs, whereas the other village was in another valley and did not have the same advantages.

ⓔ This question is worth 8 marks, which are levels based — 4 AO1 and 4 AO2. Apply your knowledge and understanding of issues from social psychology that relate to the source. Q13 in the sample assessment materials for A-level Paper 1 available on the Edexcel website has a similar levels mark scheme to what would be used here. You need to demonstrate accurate and thorough knowledge and understanding through applying it to the source and support your lines of argument with a well-developed and logical balanced answer. This extract is clearly focusing on groups, which suggests that social identity theory is a good one to choose in order to explain the extract. Using Sherif et al., you could also look at the idea that competition relates to hostility. If you have studied Tajfel's study about minimal groups, you can use the findings to help to explain the extract. The Reicher and Haslam study also looks at the success of an in-group structure, so can be used. When studying the social approach you will have looked at what the approach is about in general, such as how behaviour has to be understood in terms of groups and cultures, and those concepts can also be useful for this answer. Remember to refer to the source throughout your answer to show you are clearly focusing on the question.

Student answer

There are different theories that can explain the prejudice shown. Social identity theory (SIT) claims that prejudice arises when an in-group becomes hostile to an out-group, possibly to enhance the self-esteem of the in-group. In the source passage, the villagers in each case would probably form an in-group, including not only those who were team members but the whole village. This would be even more likely if one village were seen to be better off than the other, as was the case here. This is an example of scapegoating, which is a different concept — where people are blamed for problems they are not responsible for, and prejudice forms. Prejudice can lead to aggression through frustration, and economic disadvantages can lead to frustration. Continuing to focus on SIT, the two fighters were from different in-groups and those identifying with those in-groups backed their group showing in-group favouritism as SIT predicts. This explains why the fighting spread. There is evidence for in-group favouritism. Crocker and Luhtanen (1990) found that people who think highly of the group they are in have a high self-esteem as a group and show loyalty to their group. Lalonde (1992) found that a hockey team who knew that another hockey team was doing better nevertheless did not admit that the other team was a better team, they said that the other team used 'dirtier' tactics. In this way they could show in-group favouritism. Another theory, realistic conflict theory (RCT), would look at how the villages were fighting over resources like roads and jobs, which were scarce in the area, and that would explain the prejudice. When one group sees themselves as not having the resources and advantages of another group there is hostility and the more scarce the resources the greater the hostility and the longer it will last for. Theories can help to explain issues like the fighting in this source, however, evidence does tend to come from experiments, such as for SIT Tajfel's lab studies and for realistic group conflict theory Sherif et al.'s field study. These studies use controls and so findings might not have good validity. However, if they explain issues like the ones in this source, then they have practical application and that suggests they do have validity. If the chiefs wanted to reduce the prejudice, RCT says that they need to get the two villages working towards a superordinate goal, where to achieve it they must pull together.

e **8/8 marks awarded.** Two theories of how prejudice might occur (SIT and RCT) are given here, and each earns marks as well as the idea of scapegoating. The suggestion that frustration might cause the aggression is also useful. This links to the frustration–aggression hypothesis, which you may not have studied, but is a good, relevant point from social psychology and shows that you can bring in material from elsewhere. Further credit is given for adding that in this case, the villages were in competition, but if another situation arose where they had to work together (to solve a superordinate goal, for example), prejudice might be reduced, which links to Sherif's study. Ideas from crowd behaviour could also have been used successfully here. If you stick to what you have learned in the course, that is fine — and you could have gone into more depth about social categorisation, social comparison and social identity, using the theory if you needed to. Note that the answer is organised and the reader is led through the answer (though that could be more clear). Note too that there is evaluation about the evidence the theories rest on, towards the end, which is useful as it helps in the discussion of the concepts and ideas, though this question is not focusing on evaluation skills. The knowledge and understanding about relevant psychology (AO1) is very clear. The links between the theories and the source are very clear, too (AO2) — the application of knowledge and understanding is strong.

(2) **Social psychology can be used to help us understand key questions in psychology. Describe *one* such key question.**   (4 marks)

ⓔ This question is worth 4 AO1 marks and is points based. The main point here is to describe the issue, not the psychology that helps to explain it. Avoid mentioning studies, theories or concepts as far as you can, because they are the explanations of the issue, not the description. Sometimes you have to use concepts, because the issue is about such concepts — for example, if you choose prejudice. However, most concepts can be avoided — for example, refer to two groups in conflict, not to in-group and out-group, if you are talking about football hooliganism.

Student answer

In recent years there have been occasions when members of armed forces have been charged as individuals for brutal acts. ✓ One example is when US soldiers were photographed treating prisoners in the Abu Ghraib prison in Iraq in a humiliating and brutal way. ✓ Soldiers are supposed to treat prisoners of war carefully and with respect for their position, and there are rules and conventions. ✓ The pictures were published in the media and there was a general outcry from around the world against soldiers using their position of power in such a way. It was hard to understand how they could do this, given their training. ✓

ⓔ **4/4 marks awarded.** This answer is clear enough and marks are given quite quickly, as it is not easy to stick to describing only the issue — which is how this could happen and what would make them do it. The first mark is for the general idea that soldiers should not commit brutal acts, though this is not yet fully explained in the answer. The second mark is for the actual example. The third mark is for one side of the issue — that soldiers are not supposed to do this. The fourth mark is for the actual issue — that it is hard to understand why this would happen, with the implication that such behaviour needs to be explained.

Practical investigation

For the social approach, you will have carried out a questionnaire. Answer the following questions with your practical in mind.

(1) (a) What is the aim of the practical?   (2 marks)

ⓔ This question is worth 2 marks, which are points based and for AO1. Expect to give the aim of each of your practical investigations — the aim usually has 2 marks. Just be clear, what you were trying to find out — this often includes a brief mention of the IV and the DV, but this might not be appropriate. You do not need to give full details of these variables.

> **Student answer**
>
> My questionnaire was to find out, using both open and closed questions, if people think those in their in-group are better than others who are in the out-group. This is to test the social identity theory to see if there is in-group favouritism and if it affects self-esteem. ✓✓

ⓔ **2/2 marks awarded.** This is fine, as it gives the types of data and the independent variable (in-group answers vs out-group answers), as well as the overall aim of testing the theory and some detail about that (self-esteem and in-group favouritism).

(b) Give two examples of questions asked.   (2 marks)

ⓔ This question is worth 2 marks, which are points based and for AO1. You need to give two questions here — either open or closed questions. Here it is assumed that the practical was a questionnaire to look at social identity theory. You do not need to be exact about what you actually asked, just make sure the questions are appropriate to your aim. Of course you will answer using your own practical investigation.

> **Student answer**
>
> Do you like people in your group better than those in other groups? Yes No ✓
>
> When you are with people you don't know very well, does that make you feel less confident? Yes No ✓

ⓔ **2/2 marks awarded.** These two questions are fine and would work. You might think of problems with them, but the idea is just to test the sort of questions that could be asked and they do not have to be perfect.

(c) Why did you include or would you include personal data?   (2 marks)

ⓔ This question is worth 2 marks, which are points based and for AO1. Personal data are data about the individual rather than about the IV. The question asks you to talk about why they are needed, rather than which personal data you asked for. You could answer by referring to the actual personal data you gathered — but remember to say why.

Student answer

Personal data are needed to check the data against. For example, I asked about gender because I wanted to know if there is a gender difference in in-group preferences. ✓

(e) **1/2 marks awarded.** This gets 1 mark because the example makes the first sentence clear, but on its own the first sentence is not particularly helpful. The answer needed to say what 'check against' means. Another example might have got you another mark, if the example was detailed enough. Or the answer could say more about what personal data are.

(d) Explain one ethical decision you made.   (2 marks)

(e) This question is worth 2 marks, which are points based, and probably AO2, applying what you know about ethics to your investigation. Choose one ethical issue you considered — even if you did not address it well. Then explain the issue and what you did about it (or why you did not).

Student answer

I was careful to get informed consent. I put standardised instructions on the top of my questionnaire and said it was about in-group and out-group behaviour and that the findings would only be used for my course. I said that no names were required and that data were confidential. This told the respondent about the study, so they were informed. Then I just asked them if it was okay to continue, which meant consent was given and informed. ✓✓

(e) **2/2 marks awarded.** This is a thorough answer and gets the 2 marks.

(e) Choose whether a questionnaire is a reliable or a valid research method and explain your answer.   (2 marks)

(e) This question is worth 2 marks, which are points based and for AO3. Choose to look at either reliability or validity and then, having chosen, discuss the questionnaire research method with that issue in mind. Note that this question asks about a questionnaire in general, not about your *own* questionnaire, though you can use your own in examples to illustrate your point(s).

Student answer

A survey has good reliability because there are set questions and they are repeated for all respondents. So the answers, which often give quantitative data, can be compared and can be tested for reliability. ✓ Questions should be clear, following a pilot study, so that if they were asked again the same responses would be found, which again would show reliability. ✓

(e) **2/2 marks awarded.** This answer clearly shows understanding of what reliability is and mentions the issues of closed questions, comparability and a pilot study, all of which are useful issues with regard to reliability.

■ Cognitive psychology

Overview

(1) Describe one factor that a definition of cognitive psychology might include. (3 marks)

ⓔ This question is worth 3 marks, which are points based and for AO1. One way of getting 1 mark is to give an example that illustrates a point, but you would need to describe the factor first. Think of something about cognitive psychology in general rather than specific and write it down. Then explain it a bit more to elaborate. Then think of an example of this factor within the approach.

> **Student answer**
>
> The mind/brain processes information and cognitive psychology focuses on such processing in the brain and how it occurs. ✓ We take information in, and then it is subjected to mental processes. There is input, processing and then output. ✓ For example, we take information in via the senses, process it according to the multi-store model of memory, through three stores — the sensory register, the short-term store and the long-term store — and then there is an output if we remember the information. ✓

ⓔ **3/3 marks awarded.** This is a clear and concise answer. 1 mark is given for the factor, in this case that we process information, which is clearly given. 1 mark is awarded for linking this to the processing of information and for expanding on this by mentioning input, processing and output. There could have been 2 marks here if the idea of mental processes had been expanded as well. The example of the multi-store model gained the final mark as it is clear and used effectively. Note that just saying that the multi-store model is an example is not enough — you have to show how it is an example.

Content

(1) Assess two theories of memory in terms of the methods used to get evidence for them. (4 marks)

ⓔ This question is worth 4 marks, which are points based and for AO3. You need to focus on two theories and make it clear which they are, but you do not need to describe the theories. Your task is to look at the methods of the studies that test the theories. Be ready for questions like this, which do not look straightforward perhaps, but with a little unpacking, will become clear.

> **Student answer**
>
> Both the multi-store model and the working memory model use laboratory experiments mainly to test them. They both use recall of lists of words or letters or similar tasks and both want to see what affects recall (or recognition) of the words. ✓ The multi-store model focuses on testing rehearsal in short-term memory (STM) such as memory span (e.g. Miller's idea of 5 +/–2), which is how

many items can be recalled when long-term memory (LTM) is not in use. The working memory model also includes looking at memory span, such as digit span (e.g. Sebastián and Hernández-Gil, 2012). ✓ The working memory model, though, looks at digit span with regard to how the phonological loop works, which is not quite the same as the experiments testing the multi-store model and looking at either STM or LTM. ✓ Then again it can be claimed that rehearsal is done using the phonological loop so the theories fit quite well together and it is not surprising that the methods used are so similar. ✓

ⓔ **4/4 marks awarded.** This answer focuses throughout on the methods. It begins with the main research method and examples of what experiments might focus on (assesses, says 'both'). Then the focus is on method, again by showing that memory span experiments are carried out and giving examples (assesses, says 'also'). There is another mark for showing the different focus of the experiments because of them testing two different theories (assesses, says 'not quite the same as'). The last mark is at the end, showing that as the theories fit together it is not surprising the methods are similar (assesses, says 'similar').

(2) Evaluate *one* theory or model of memory in terms of *two* of the following criteria: methodological issues, ethical issues, alternative theories, research evidence for contradictory claims or its practical application. (4 marks)

ⓔ This question is worth 4 marks, which are points based and for AO3. You have to do two things here and there are 4 marks, so assume there are 2 marks for each criterion. Choose one of the criteria (e.g. ethical issues) and say three things about ethical issues in relation to your chosen theory of memory. Then choose one of the other criteria (e.g. alternative theories) and say three things about alternative theories. You can get marks by elaborating a point, so, for example, if you choose ethics and talk about one ethical issue in depth, you could gain more than 1 mark, or you could gain marks by looking at different ethical issues. You should add a conclusion.

Student answer

The multi-store model has stimulated much research into the mind to identify exactly how memory is used and stored. This stimulated research by Baddeley and Hitch, who came up with the working memory (WM) model. ✓ The WM model expands short-term memory (STM) to look at different areas. These include an articulatory loop, a visuospatial sketchpad and a central executive. ✓ Research is based on experimental evidence, which is said to lack validity as artificial tasks are used (such as lists of words). ✓

ⓔ **3/4 marks awarded.** The first criterion covered is alternative theory, and for this 2 marks are gained. 1 mark is for the mention of the model having stimulated research such as the working memory model. The second mark is for mentioning the areas of the working model, and elaborating on this. The second criterion is methodological issues, and a mark is given for mentioning the artificial nature of experiments used. This could have been explained more fully, for the final 2 marks. There is mention of using lists of words and more could be said for the mark, such as how Baddeley (1966b) used lists of 10 words and asked for recall in order, which is not that natural. Adding 'using lists of words' comes very close to getting the other mark for that criterion, but is not quite enough.

(3) For *one* model/theory of memory that you have studied, copy and complete the following table. (3 marks)

Instruction regarding the model or theory	Answer
Identify the model/theory	
State one aspect of the model/theory	
Explain one problem with the model/theory	

ⓔ There is 1 mark for each element. The first and second marks are AO1 and the last is likely to be AO3. The first mark is for naming the model (or identifying it if you cannot recall the name of the theory or the name(s) of the researcher(s)). The second mark is for saying something about that model — for example, if looking at the multi-store model, saying that the focus is on two stores: STM and LTM. The third mark is for saying something to criticise it.

Student answer

Instruction regarding the model or theory	Answer
Identify the model/theory	Reconstructive memory, Baddeley (1932)
State one aspect of the model/theory	Recall involves reconstruction rather than exact recall as schemas interfere while processing
Explain one problem with the model/theory	Tends to be tested using artificial tasks, such as the complicated 'War of the Ghosts' story. When tasks are more natural, as Steyvers and Hemmer (2012) show, there is less reconstruction and more 'accuracy'

ⓔ **3/3 marks awarded.** Each of the above answers scores 1 mark.

Method (also A-level Paper 3)

(1) Explain *one* strength and *one* weakness of the experiment as a research method. (4 marks)

ⓔ There are 2 marks for the strength and 2 marks for the weakness — they are for AO3 and points based. Do not just give a brief answer for each: be sure to expand it enough for the full 2 marks. For example, say what the strength is and then justify what you mean. This is not about a particular experiment, it is about the research method itself.

Student answer

A strength is that it is well controlled. A weakness is that you cannot see natural behaviour, as the experiment is in a laboratory. ✓

ⓔ 1/4 marks awarded. The strength does not earn a mark. The answer needs to say *what* is well controlled, and how that means that a study can be repeated to see if the same results are found, which means it has reliability, or at least something about why good controls are a strength. The weakness gets 1 mark because the answer clearly and effectively communicates that natural behaviour is not found in a laboratory. For the additional mark, this needs elaborating, perhaps mentioning the lack of validity, or saying that the unnatural situation means that what is being measured is not 'normal' and that the laboratory situation is artificial because of the controls.

(2) Here are some data from a study.

Table 1 Number of words recognised in the right order from a list of 10 words depending on whether the words sound alike or do not sound alike

Participant	Recall of words that sound alike	Recall of words that do not sound alike
1	3	7
2	4	9
3	2	10
4	6	5
5	5	6
6	4	8
Mean	4	7.5
Median	–	–
Mode	4	–
Range	4	5

(a) Work out the median for the two sets of scores. (2 marks)

ⓔ This question is worth 2 marks, which are points based and for AO2. These are maths marks and you should expect 10% of maths in your course overall in the exam papers. Work out the median for each set. You will be able to take a calculator into the examination.

Student answer

The median for the 'sound alike' condition is 4. ✓

The median for the other condition (do not sound alike) is 7.5. ✓

ⓔ 2/2 marks awarded. 1 mark for each median as they are correct. It is necessary to give the right answer (e.g. not 'between 7 and 8' for the 'do not sound alike' condition).

(b) Is the set of scores for the 'sound alike' condition normally distributed? Explain your answer. (2 marks)

ⓔ This question is worth 2 marks, which are points based and for AO2. The marks are not for giving a 'yes' or 'no' answer — the 2 marks are for justifying whether you claim 'yes' or 'no'.

The mean, median and mode are all 4 in the 'sound alike' condition and so there would be normal distribution, yes. ✓ There is normal distribution if the scores cluster evenly around the mean average and if the mode and median are the same, then that does mean the scores are evenly clustered. Also there is no outlier score, as can be seen by looking at the scores themselves. ✓

ⓔ 2/2 marks awarded. The first sentence is the main answer, but you need more for the second mark — and this answer gives more, talking about no outlier and how normal distribution means clustering around the middle.

Studies

(1) Assess the study by Baddeley (1966b) in terms of its usefulness in giving evidence for short-term and long-term memory being different. (8 marks)

(Also A-level Paper 3)

ⓔ This is a levels-based question involving AO1 (knowledge and understanding) and AO3 (comments about its usefulness in relation to STM and LTM). Note that you need to describe what was done in the study as well as evaluating its usefulness. You can see the level descriptors in the sample assessment materials on the Edexcel website — look for an 'assess' question for 8 marks (e.g. Q14, A-level Paper 1). You need to present a logical piece of writing, which is well-expressed and uses key terms. You need to show accurate and thorough knowledge with understanding, logical chains of reasoning and an awareness of the significance of competing arguments leading to a balanced judgement.

Student answer A

Baddeley (1966b) knew from other studies that STM used acoustic processing and he wanted to see if that was the case for LTM as well. He devised a study using a list of 10 words that sounded alike and a control list to match those words but without 'sound alike' words. He had in another condition a list of 10 words with similar meaning and also a control list. His idea was to see if participants would recall the order of the words (and the words) better with or without acoustic similarity or with or without semantic similarity. If STM is likely to mean better recall with semantic similarity (acoustic similarity would confuse) then if LTM is like STM that would happen in LTM too. He used an independent groups design with four groups. For each list he showed the 10 words in a measured way one at a time and then asked for recall of the words in order. He recorded number of words recalled in the right position. Then he gave the participant a 20-minute task. After that he asked for recall again, this was the re-test. He therefore had 5 scores for each participant for each task. There were 4 scores that were more or less immediate and then the re-test score. For each condition (acoustic similarity and semantic similarity) he drew up a graph to show the results against their control list. He used three experiments, so he could rule out use of STM in the study — he wanted to see what coding was used in LTM. His results showed that in LTM the acoustically similar list recall in the 'similar' condition and the control condition was very similar, including at re-test, so acoustic similarity gave few issues. In the semantically similar list recall was better in the control condition. He concluded that long-term memory is affected by semantic similarity but not by acoustic similarity. This is different from what is found in short-term memory, where acoustic similarity is more problematic. This is evidence that LTM uses semantic coding (which compares with evidence from other studies that STM uses acoustic coding). Baddeley (1966b) showed that coding in STM is different from coding in LTM.

With regard to usefulness, Baddeley did show LTM and STM differences and also backed up other studies showing STM relies on acoustic coding, so the body of knowledge is being built up. However, this was an experiment using lists of 10 words and so validity is in doubt. This is not a very real-life situation, not only being an experiment but also because learning lists is not a natural situation. Knowing about how memory works can help people with dementia, for example, and can help with learning, so there are practical applications, which is useful. For example, case studies like HM showed how STM can be affected when LTM is not, so showing they are different backs up neurological evidence (e.g. the role of the hippocampus) and is useful. To conclude, it would seem that there are more usefulness points than the study showing a lack of usefulness.

e **6/8 marks awarded.** This is a good answer with regard to knowledge and understanding, so the top mark in Level 3 would be given. However, it would probably only receive 6 marks as the 'usefulness' discussion, though good, perhaps needs a bit more focus — the balance is not quite there. There is so much good detail with regard to the study, clearly in the time all that could be written, but the argument about usefulness could be developed more. The comment about helping with dementia could be extended to discuss the importance of sound and rehearsal when using STM and there could be mention of how knowing STM and LTM are different in coding supports the idea of working memory expanding understanding of STM (with its focus on the phonological loop and visual spatial sketchpad rather than meaning).

Student answer B

Baddeley (1966b) did a study looking at STM and LTM and used lists of words with differences to see the differences between them. He used an experiment, which was not valid but had reliability. He found that LTM was better than STM and this is useful because then we know the difference and can use the information in society. He found that LTM was for meaning and STM for sound, which was the main difference.

e **1/8 marks awarded.** This answer is clearly not enough for the top level. You can get the idea of STM and LTM, and the link to 'differences' from the title. There are two knowledge points, though they do not show understanding — one saying that the study was an experiment and one linking STM to sound and LTM to meaning. There is an evaluation point, linking experiments to reliability and validity, but this also does not show understanding. There is a comment about his distinction between STM and LTM being useful for society but more needs to be said. The mark scheme for Q14, sample assessment materials, A-level Paper 1, helps to show what Level 1 requires. Level 1 for an 'assess' 8-mark question is for demonstrating isolated elements of knowledge and understanding, showing a limited attempt to address the question, and giving generic assertions. This answer therefore fits into Level 1.

(2) Using one of the studies you have covered listed in cognitive psychology in your course, explain one way the results were analysed. (3 marks)

🅔 This question is worth 3 marks, which are points based and for AO1, though 'explain' can involve some AO3. You can choose any of the studies listed in this part of the course: the classic study, Baddeley (1966b), or one of the three contemporary studies — Schmolck et al. (2002), Steyvers and Hemmer (2012) or Sebastián and Hernández-Gil (2012). Pick out something about how the results were analysed for one of these studies. 'Explain' means give one way the results were analysed and then justify your answer for the second and third marks. This question shows that you need a good understanding of the studies, in some depth.

Student answer

Baddeley (1966b) used both the Mann–Whitney U and Wilcoxon tests and one of these is explained here. He used the Mann–Whitney U test to look at differences between the different participants, one group who were the control group in Experiment 3 and one who had the words that had similar meaning. ✓The data were interval, being the number of words recalled in the right order from 10. The design was independent groups. Baddeley was looking for a difference between these two groups. ✓ The test for difference independent groups design and interval data in the course is Mann–Whitney U, which statistically compares differences between the two groups. ✓

🅔 **3/3 marks awarded.** There is a clear analysis point — that Mann–Whitney U was used to analyse the data. Then a really good justification for the two other marks, so full marks given. The reader knows exactly how the results were analysed (one way) and what this meant. Note there was no need to give the actual results. However, the answer could have considered the level of significance chosen. Note that the answer identifies the study, which is sensible.

Key question

(1) To what extent can concepts, theories and studies in cognitive psychology explain one key question you have studied within cognitive psychology? (8 marks, essay)

🅔 The marks here are given in levels from an answer that gives no rewardable material (0 marks) to an answer that is well detailed and well focused on the question, giving both description and evaluation. The 8 marks will include AO1 and AO3. You should describe the key question so that it is clear which key question you are explaining and why it is a key question for society. Then you should give research — concepts, theories and studies — from cognitive psychology to show how far psychology can explain the key question. Evaluation will be needed as part of this discussion. You must come to a judgement in your answer.

How understanding of memory helps in dementia is a key question for society as incidents of dementia are rising in the UK and there are costs to society. These costs are not only financial costs but personal costs as well. The more those with dementia can be helped and supported, the better for them and for society. A key question is how to offer such help and support and how psychology can advise. Psychology studies memory a lot and there are four main models of memory. These are the multi-store model, the theory of memory being reconstructed, the working memory model and the idea of there being episodic and semantic memories in long-term memory. Those with dementia can be helped by using their episodic memories and jogging them, such as setting up scenes they would be familiar with in their lives. This can make them feel less confused.

Also memory tests can help to identify dementia, such as checking memory span. The multi-store model says that memory span is about 7 items. If someone has a span of nearer 5 (and there would have to be other issues too), then, as Sebastián and Hernández-Gil (2012) say, that would match what would be expected from someone with dementia. Working memory says that it is hard to process information if sense data are incoming using the same mode, such as using sound, but more than one source. Therefore, it is helpful to avoid too much information for someone with dementia and giving them time to process one source of information at a time, such as not having a radio on if speaking to someone with dementia. Three models of memory are used here to show how they are useful for someone with dementia. Studies like Baddeley's (1966b) one support models of memory. The models are helpful for members of society, studies support them, and they explain the key question well.

🅔 **5/8 marks awarded.** This question is marked using levels. There is clearly knowledge with understanding of the key question but not much detail about the numbers of those with dementia or other such information to show why this is a contemporary and key question. Nevertheless, the key question is set out and the idea of it being important for society is outlined. There is also good knowledge and understanding of the memory models. These are not detailed, but the answer is about how psychological understanding can help people with dementia and that is what this answer talks about, rather than describing the models. There are lines of argument and they are supported by evidence in one case. The answer is well written and logically presented. Perhaps more evidence would be useful and more discussion, such as Baddeley's (1966b) study as evidence of the issues with the phonological loop. This answer is not quite in the top level. It is mostly coherent, there is some evidence, the knowledge and understanding is here though perhaps not thorough, so Level 3 seems a good choice. This can be 5 or 6 marks. 5 marks are given here, because the answer is a bit list-like with three ideas for helping those with dementia. Use Q14, A-level Paper 1, sample assessment materials, which you can find on the Edexcel website, to check the level descriptors for yourself for this type of question.

Practical investigation

Within cognitive psychology you will have carried out an experiment on some aspect of either memory or forgetting.

(1) (a) Give the aim of your study. (1 mark)

ⓔ There is 1 AO1 mark available for a clearly stated aim. The study on which we focus here for answers is based on a study similar to Peterson and Peterson, 1959, which focuses on testing short-term memory. You should answer this section using the practical you did for your own course. Use the comments and answers here to see what is required.

Student answer

The aim was to see if participants who had an interference task when recalling a list of letters presented randomly recalled fewer words than if there was rehearsal time (no interference). ✓

ⓔ **1/1 mark awarded.** This is fine and clear.

(b) Explain one control that you put into place, other than sampling or standardised instructions. (2 marks)

ⓔ This question is worth 2 marks, which are points based and for AO1. There are situational and participant variables that need to be controlled in an experiment. Sampling and standardised instructions control participant variables so consider another participant variable or a situational variable for your own study.

Student answer

One control is that the letters being recalled are the same for everyone, including being typed the same and in the same order, ✓ using the same timing for recall (whether there is an interference task or not).

ⓔ **1/2 marks awarded.** This is not easy to mark. It would be better to stick to one clear control. Here one control is about the letters used (this is the apparatus) and the other is to do with a different part of the procedure, the timing. The examiner will see if the two can be linked — asking, in this case, whether the timing is about control over apparatus or not. It is better not to leave it to an examiner to work out this sort of thing — be clear. The other mark is not given here. To get 2 marks for this answer, you need to stick to the apparatus and explain that letters are not in their order and no sense can be made from them, and this is the case for both conditions. At least then you are still talking about the letters.

(c) Explain how you gave (or could have given) your participants the right to withdraw. (3 marks)

ⓔ There are 3 AO1 marks available (points based) for explaining how the right to withdraw was given. This means that good detail is required.

Student answer

Standardised instructions were read out to all participants just before they started to complete the experiment. The instructions thanked everyone in advance for their cooperation and informed them clearly that, at that point, they could withdraw from the study. ✓ The instructions went on to say that each participant could withdraw from the study at any time and would be able to withdraw their data at the end if they wished to. ✓ At the end of the study the participants were thanked again and asked again if their data could be used, and they were reminded that they could withdraw their data if they wished. ✓ Nobody did and all seemed happy to have taken part.

e **3/3 marks awarded.** This gets the full 3 marks because there is quite a bit of depth. Note that you have to make your points clearly to get the marks.

(d) What was the independent variable and how did you operationalise it? (3 marks)

e This question is worth 3 marks, which are points based and for AO1. The IV is usually fully operationalised, but you could give a general IV for this answer first, as you then have to show how it is operationalised anyway. The IV might not get a mark until it is operationalised when given as an answer to another question, but as there are 3 marks here for the IV, detail is needed.

Student answer

The IV was the participant had to do an interference task or not. ✓ This was operationalised based largely on Peterson and Peterson. The interference task involved counting backwards from a three digit number, such as 389, in threes (such as 389, 386, 383...). ✓The interference task lasted 30 seconds so the other condition was to wait for 30 seconds (when rehearsal could take place). ✓ The IV was, therefore, whether the participant had the interference task of counting backwards in threes from a number they were given for 30 seconds or not. (✓)

e **3/3 marks awarded.** This answer gets all 3 marks and there was enough for a fourth mark if it had been needed. The first mark was for a rather brief but accurate IV, but then marks were given for more information. There are two points in this study about operationalising the IV, one is the actual interference task and the other is how long it lasts for. Both are explained well here.

Issues and debates (A-level only, Papers 1 and 3)

(1) Evaluate practical issues in the design of studies, focusing on studies in both social and cognitive psychology in your answer. (12 marks)

e This question is worth 12 marks (AO1 and AO3) and it is levels based. You need to describe practical issues in how studies are designed and use examples from both social and cognitive psychology. The main focus is to discuss such practical issues, focusing on strengths and weaknesses and coming to a judgement at the end, which is evaluating as the question asks. You could choose two studies, one from social and one from cognitive, and consider practical issues in their design, evaluating the issues. Be sure to focus on practical issues.

Student answer

Sherif et al (1954/1961) used a field study to find out about prejudice, how it forms and how it can be reduced. Baddeley (1966b) used laboratory experiments to look at what mode of representation is used in long-term memory. Design decisions would be different for each and each would involve different practical issues. Sherif et al (1954/1961) had to focus on sampling and being sure that there were two groups that were well-matched so that prejudice could not come from individual differences, but came from the situation. They had to match the participants in the first place, and then match them again when they split them into two groups. This was because they needed an independent groups design, because the groups had to know nothing about one another at the start.

However, they needed the two groups to have no individual differences, so the sampling was important. Matching two groups has practical problems, because there are so many variables to consider. Sherif et al. matched IQ and teachers rated the boys. They also looked at home background, which must have been hard to do (it is hard to make sure there are not problems 'at home'). They chose boys as a design decision, to take care of gender issues, which helped to make practical problems easier. Baddeley had fewer problems with the sampling because he could take more or less any age (adults) and any background and IQ. He also had an independent groups design though, so you could say there might be individual differences causing any differences he found in processing, but he could use a lot of participants and the DV did not depend on their previous knowledge and so on, as it did for Sherif et al. (such as the boys not knowing about each other's existence).

A field study perhaps makes it harder to find and sort out the participants whereas a laboratory study can often use those available. Milgram used an independent groups design in his study too, though his study did not really have two parts to the independent variable, he just used one participant at a time. He did not take a long time sorting his participants out, he accepted volunteers, so just like Baddeley, the lab experiment research method perhaps needs less focus on sampling and design decisions in the sense of which participants are used. However, Burger (2009) did take a lot of trouble in screening his participants in his replication of Milgram, because of ethical issues. Perhaps it is not so much different design decisions in social and cognitive psychology, but practical issues in design decisions depend on what the aims of the study are and the research method chosen as well as other issues like ethics.

ⓔ **12/12 marks awarded.** This answer shows accurate and thorough knowledge and understanding (in the time available for a 12-mark answer), which is in the top level. You can refer to the levels in the sample answer materials for A-level Paper 1 (found on the Edexcel website) Q15. There are lines of argument supported by relevant evidence and both social and cognitive psychology are involved in the answer. Four studies are mentioned and it is clear they are known. Knowledge is used to answer the question and there is not 'pure' description, which is effective for this question (given time limits). There is also a logical progression through the argument, with good chains of reasoning shown. It is evaluated well and there is a good clear conclusion, showing focus on the question.

Glossary

The social approach

Agency theory Milgram's explanation for obedience to those in authority. He thought that being in an agentic state would benefit society and so might be a behaviour that was handed down through natural selection.

Agentic state the state people are in when they are acting as agents for someone else or society rather than acting according to their own principles and their own decisions.

Aim what the researcher wants to find out.

Alternate hypothesis the statement of what is expected in a study, such as 'young females who have just passed their test are better drivers around a prescribed course than young males who have just passed their test'.

Authoritarian personality people rigid in their thinking, liking rules in society, obeying those rules, seeing the world in black and white.

Autonomous state the state people are in when they are acting for themselves and making their own decisions, as opposed to being in an agentic state.

Closed-ended (closed) questions questions that ask for specific responses, where the answers are restrained by boxes or categories of replies such as yes/no answers or ratings on a scale.

Competence one of the four ethical principles in the BPS Code of Ethics and Conduct (2009). It involves researchers only working at their level of competence, including keeping up-to-date in their area.

Conditions aspects of the IV that are varied, such as gender (male and female) and in-group preference.

Construct validity the questions measure what the hypothesis or research question needs, so if the claim is that questions measure in-group preferences, there is construct validity only if they do so.

Controls procedures in a study that make sure that what is done and measured is not affected by external factors such as noise, time of day, temperature, bias from the researcher or anything else. If a study is carefully and well controlled then findings are secure — they are about what they say they are about. Controls are put in place to avoid bias.

Credibility is found when controls are good, the study is carefully run, there is objectivity and reliability and so the scientific community will accept the findings as being believable.

Data results and findings from studies of any sort. Data are what are gathered from a study and can be either qualitative or quantitative.

Debrief an explanation given at the end of a study to a participant, saying what the study was about, what results were expected and how the results will be used. It gives the participant the chance to ask questions and the right to withdraw their data. It is part of the principle of responsibility.

Deception part of the principle of integrity. Participants in a study should not be deceived. Athough this might be necessary, it should be minimal and a debrief must tell participants about any deception and check all is well.

Deindividuation the idea that people can become unidentifiable as individuals in certain situations, such as when wearing a uniform or when in a crowd. People can then act in ways in which they would not normally act because their control over themselves as individuals is to an extent lost.

Demand characteristic a feature of a study that gives a clue about what is intended, so that participants can either try to help the researcher by doing what they think is wanted or be unhelpful. Either way data are not valid so the study is not a good one. It is a form of bias.

Dependent variable (DV) what is being measured — what changes as a result of the manipulation of the independent variable.

Discrimination an action arising from a prejudiced attitude.

Ecological validity the questions measure what the hypothesis or research question needs, and if the setting and situation (the 'ecology') is not natural then data are not going to be 'real life'.

Ethics principles of right and wrong with regard to the actions of others or of societies, and issues concerning right and wrong. There are ethical guidelines for the treatment of both human and animal participants of studies. Researchers need to make sure that studies with human participants do not upset anyone and that everyone is treated fairly and with respect.

Experimental hypothesis the alternate hypothesis for an experiment (i.e. for any other research method it is called the alternate hypothesis). The experimental hypothesis is the statement of what is expected in an experiment, such as 'more words from a list are recalled if they are learnt in categories than if learnt as a random list'.

Generalisability the sampling works and the target population is represented by the sample used.

Hypothesis the statement of what is expected when a test or study is to be carried out. The alternate or experimental hypothesis says what is expected while the null hypothesis says the opposite — that any results found in a study will not be significant enough to draw conclusions and are likely to be due to chance. Statistical tests look to see if results are significant enough to be unlikely to be due to chance.

Independent variable (IV) what the researcher manipulates in a study. There are usually two conditions (or more) in the study.

Informed consent the agreement of participants to take part in a study on the basis that they know what the study is about, and the principle that they must be given this information before taking part. It is part of the principle of respect.

Internal validity any cause-and-effect conclusion is the case. If there are confounding variables in that the IV was not what caused the change in the DV then this means there is no internal validity.

In-group the group that someone categorises themselves as belonging to.

Integrity one of the four ethical principles in the BPS Code of Ethics and Conduct (2009). It involves researchers being honest in their work including what they publish and how they handle boundaries with others. Integrity involves lack of deception in research.

Interview a way of collecting data by asking spoken questions. Structured interviews have a set of questions that are stuck to. Semi-structured interviews involve some set questions but some allowance for exploring issues. Unstructured interviews involve an interview schedule or set of questions but then the interviewer can explore different areas that arise according to the respondent's answers.

Interviewee a person being interviewed. The participant in an interview is called the interviewee and the participant in a questionnaire is called the respondent.

Likert-type data a rating scale that uses categories for gathering data. There might be five points on a scale, for example: 'strongly agree', 'agree', 'unsure', 'disagree', 'strongly disagree'.

Mean a measure of central tendency (average) that is calculated by totalling the scores and then dividing by how many scores there are. It is only useful for data at the interval/ratio level of measurement.

Measures of central tendency averages, which include the mode, median and mean.

Measures of dispersion measures of how the data are spread around the mean. The range is a measure of dispersion, as is the standard deviation.

Median a measure of central tendency (average) that is worked out by finding the middle score. If there is no middle score the median is midway between the two either side of the middle. For example, out of ten scores the median is between the fifth and sixth score.

Methodology a set of research methods and everything to do with them.

Mode a measure of central tendency (average) that is worked out by finding the most common score. If there is more than one 'most common' score, then all are given. For example, if there are two modal scores, the data set is bi-modal.

Moral strain the pressure of doing something against one's own moral code.

Natural selection according to evolution theory, the passing on of any tendency that aids survival. If an organism with a particular characteristic survives to reproduce, the genes causing that characteristic are passed on.

Null hypothesis the statement that the difference or relationship predicted to happen in a study will not happen. For example, 'young female drivers who have just passed their test will not be better drivers around a prescribed course than young male drivers'. The null hypothesis acknowledges that there might still be a difference in the driving of the two genders but any difference there is will not be large enough to conclude that the difference in driving is because of the difference in gender. The difference could be due to chance or to another factor not considered. A statistical test looks to see if a difference that is found is likely to be due to chance. If the test shows that the difference is large enough for it to be unlikely to be due to chance, then the null hypothesis (which says there is not a large enough difference) will be rejected and the alternate hypothesis (which says there is a difference) will be accepted.

Obedience obeying someone in authority (an authority figure).

Objectivity not allowing personal views to affect analysis, so that findings are relevant, reliable and valid. Science requires objectivity because if factors about a researcher affect results, then the results cannot be used to build a body of knowledge.

Open-ended (open) questions asking for people's opinions and attitudes in a way that allows them to write whatever they like, without being limited in any way.

Operationalisation making the variables of interest measurable and testable.

Opportunity sampling the researcher takes whoever is available to take part in the study. The sample is sometimes called a grab or convenience sample.

Out-group the other group, when someone categorises themselves as being in the in-group. Those in the in-group become prejudiced and discriminate against the out-group.

Participant the person providing the data in a study — the person taking part. The participant used to be called the 'subject' until it was realised that this made them more like an 'object' than an individual with a part in the study.

Participant variables variables in the participant that should be controlled for such as tiredness or gender.

Personal data information about respondents such as their age, gender, occupation, whether they have a driving licence — whatever is of interest.

Personality individual differences in behaviour, thinking and emotions, involving traits that are relatively stable over time and responses to certain situations that can be predicted, giving such traits. An example is the Big Five.

Pilot study a small-scale practice run of a task or survey to find out any problems and put them right before the real thing.

Glossary

Predictive validity when a study's results predict real-life behaviour/results of another study.

Prejudice a negative attitude towards someone or a group that results in stereotyping. Prejudice can be positive but is usually negative. Any negative attitude based on uncertain facts is a prejudiced attitude.

Prior consent consent to taking part in a study in cases where participants are asked in general if they would be volunteers for a study without knowing exactly what it is about.

Qualitative data opinions and attitudes that are gathered and analysed rather than set answers. In a questionnaire qualitative data are gathered by open-ended questions.

Quantitative data data gathered in the form of numbers, such as numbers of yes/no answers, and measurable categories, such as ratings on a scale of 0 to 10. In a questionnaire quantitative data are gathered by closed-ended questions.

Random sampling everyone in the chosen population has an equal chance of being in the sample.

Range a measure of dispersion. The range is calculated by taking the lowest score from the highest score. Sometimes you have to take 1 away from that calculation to get the range.

Ranked data data that come from rankings such as a rating for attractiveness from 0 to 10.

Reliability the extent to which the same (or very similar) data are yielded when a test or study is run again. If data from a repeat of the study are very similar, then the study is said to give reliable results. If they were not reliable, findings from the study could not be added to a scientific body of knowledge.

Representative sample a sample in which everyone in the target population is represented. For example, if the target population includes all females, then females of every age should be part of the sample, and perhaps females with different educational backgrounds and different jobs.

Researcher effects where some aspect of the researcher(s) affects data such as their age, the way they dress or how they ask questions.

Respect one of the four ethical principles in the BPS Code of Ethics and Conduct (2009). It involves getting informed consent, giving the right to withdraw, and respecting privacy and confidentiality.

Respondent the person giving the answers in a survey; the participant.

Response bias factors in the question or task giving a bias, such as tending to suggest the answer 'yes' and thereafter getting that answer regardless; or bias in the respondent, such as having the type of personality that tends to agree or disagree. Such people may try to be helpful, for example, and say what they think is wanted.

Response set either getting into the habit of answering in a particular way (such as 'yes') to a set of questions and so continuing in that way regardless. This can happen if a Likert-type scale is used and all the statements are phrased so that 'strongly agree' is in the same direction (such as being prejudiced). Such statements should be mixed so that sometimes a prejudiced person would answer 'strongly disagree'. A particular type of response bias.

Responsibility one of the four ethical principles in the BPS Code of Ethics and Conduct (2009). It involves debriefing participants after a study, and being responsible for their welfare throughout. This principle is about avoiding harm and not 'looking away'.

Right to withdraw giving participants throughout a study the right to stop taking part. It is part of the principle of respect.

Sampling the way people are chosen to take part in a study. Usually not all the people being studied can be involved, so there has to be a sample.

Sampling frame the people chosen from which the sampling is done. The whole target population cannot usually be chosen, so there is a suitable sampling frame, such as one primary school to represent all primary schools.

Schedule in an interview, the list of questions, any instructions, and any other information such as the length of time for the interview.

Science building a body of knowledge in such a way that others can rely on the knowledge. This involves objectivity, measurable concepts (so that the tests can be done again), careful controls and the generating of hypotheses from previous theory (so that one piece of evidence can link to another one to build the knowledge).

Self-rating giving a rating score about oneself, such as for attractiveness or meanness.

Semi-structured interview has some set questions though the respondent can still take the lead to an extent and the interviewer can follow the answers up as they can in an unstructured interview.

Simple random sampling a method of sampling by which everyone in the sampling frame or target population has an equal chance of being chosen to be included in the sample.

Situational variables are variables in the situation that should be controlled for such as the weather.

Social categorisation a process of accepting oneself as being part of an in-group, according to social identity theory.

Social comparison the process of comparing one's in-group with the out-group and thinking of the in-group as better in some way. This enhances the individual's self-esteem and can lead to prejudice.

Social desirability the tendency we have to say what we think we ought to say or do what we ought to do in a given situation. For example, it is socially desirable to say we recycle rubbish so a survey is likely to find that we do — even if we do not — because we are likely to say that we do. It is a form of bias.

Social identification a process of identifying with an in-group after categorising oneself as being part of the in-group.

Social impact refers to the effect of others, in particular groups, on our attitudes and can lead to obedience when otherwise someone might not obey.

Standard deviation a measure of dispersion that you can learn about for your course, but you do not have to. The standard deviation is worked out by taking all the scores away from the mean average to see how far the scores fluctuate around the mean. Whether they fluctuate or not can show how far they are spread around the mean average, which helps when interpreting the data.

Stereotyping transferring an opinion about an individual onto other individuals or groups.

Stratified sampling a method of sampling by which the target population is divided into required groups or strata, and corresponding proportions of people from these groups are picked out for the sample.

Structured interview has all the questions set out and all respondents are asked the same questions in the same format.

Subjectivity allowing personal views to affect analysis so that findings are affected.

Superordinate goal a goal that can only be reached by two (or more) groups working together to achieve it.

Target population all the people the results will be applied to when the study is done.

Thematic analysis is a way of getting qualitative data into something that is manageable for reporting on and involves generating themes from the data using categories and the grouping of ideas.

Transcript is a complete typing up of the data in full, ready for analysis, and applies to qualitative data.

Unstructured interview has a schedule but not a set of questions set out fully. The respondent can take more of the lead.

Validity the extent to which a test or study yields data that apply to a real-life setting and real-life situations; the extent to which the data are 'true'. If a study is measuring what it claims to measure (for example, if it has really found out about prejudice, and not just what we think we should say about prejudice) then it is said to give valid results. If they were not valid, findings from the study could not be added to a scientific body of knowledge.

Volunteer/self-selected sampling a method of sampling by which people are asked to volunteer for the study either personally or via an advertisement. They self-select themselves by volunteering.

The cognitive approach

Articulatory loop in the working memory model, within the phonological loop, and for speech, such as using rehearsal to put information into long-term memory.

Baseline measure a measure of what would 'normally' be the case so that in an experiment a difference can be tested for. It comes from the control group; the researcher compares the control group with the experimental group to see what difference the experiment has made.

Capacity size in the multi-store model of memory, the size of a store and the storage space available.

Central executive according to the working memory model, it is the controller of the system. It controls the flow of information and the processing; for example, it gets information into one stream, and controls whether the phonological loop or visuospatial scratchpad is needed.

Chi-squared the statistical test used when difference is looked for and an independent design used, with nominal data.

Computer analogy the idea that the brain can be likened to a computer, with input (from the senses), throughput (the processing) and output.

Conditions parts or aspects of the independent variable, such as whether words are in capitals (visual), whether they rhyme (auditory) or whether they fit into a sentence correctly (semantic).

Confabulation making up bits of an event when retelling it so that it makes more sense, which means a memory is not exactly like the perception of the event.

Confounding variables extraneous variables that seem to have affected the results of a study. For example, in a study memory was found to be better when recall was in the same context as learning; but in practice it was found that all those studied in the same context were younger than those studied in a different context, so age would be a confounding variable.

Control group the group in an experiment that is producing a baseline measure of what would 'normally' happen without the manipulated condition in the experiment, such as learning a random list of letters rather than a grouped list and trying to recall them.

Counterbalancing alternating the conditions for each participant in an experiment to help to control for order effects in a repeated measures design. If there are two conditions, for example, the first participant does condition one followed by condition two. Then the second participant does condition two followed by condition one and so on.

Demand characteristics characteristics found when participants' responses are affected by their guessing what the study is about.

Glossary

Dependent variable (DV) what is being measured as a result of the experiment and as a result of the independent variable being manipulated. For example, when doing an experiment looking at the effect of interference on short-term memory in the number of letters recalled, the dependent variable of a study would be how many letters are recalled.

Directional hypothesis a hypothesis that predicts the direction of the results, such as whether more or fewer words are recalled. For example, 'recall of letters is greater if letters are grouped (chunked) than if they are not'.

Duration the time something lasts. In the multi-store model it refers to how long a memory can stay in a store until it is lost (or the trace decays).

Ecological validity the extent to which the setting of a study is real life. If the setting is a natural one then the study has ecological validity and in that sense the findings are about real life. However, if the setting is not natural, as in a laboratory experiment, then the study lacks ecological validity, and the findings might not be about real life.

Encoding the first part of memory. Material has to be taken into the brain and held there somehow. Information comes from sense data and encoding can be visual, auditory or semantic — and perhaps in other forms such as touch. Encoding is about registering the information.

Episodic memory memory for episodes and events in our lives — splits semantic memory into this as well as memory of meaning.

Experimental group the group in an experiment which is doing the condition that is of interest, such as learning grouped letters and then trying to recall them rather than a randomised list.

Experimenter effects features of the researcher that affect the results of a study, such as tone of voice or facial expression. These might lead the participants to react in certain ways.

Extraneous variables things that might affect the results of a study instead of or as well as the independent variable, such as noise, heat, light or some characteristic of the participants.

Fatigue effect an order effect that occurs when the first part or condition of a study is done better than a later one because the participants are tired by the time they do the second condition.

Field experiment an experiment with as many controls as possible and a manipulated independent variable, but conducted in the field rather than in a lab situation. In the field means in the participant's natural setting.

Independent variable (IV) what is being manipulated by the researcher. This is what is of interest in the study, and what is being tested. For example, when doing an experiment looking at the effect of interference on short-term memory in the number of letters recalled, the independent variable would be whether there is interference in the task or not.

Information processing the way that information comes into the brain via the senses, has something done to it (i.e. it is processed) and then there is an output in some form. There is a flow of information into, through, and out of the brain. This is what the cognitive approach is all about.

Interval/ratio a level of measurement where data are real measurements such as time or temperature. A mean average is suitable.

Laboratory experiment an experiment in a controlled setting that is also artificial, i.e. not in the participant's natural environment. In a lab experiment, there is often an experimental group and a control group, standardised instructions and good control over all variables other than the independent variable.

Levels of measurement ways in which data are scored or measured. There are three main levels of measurement for psychology at AS and A-level: nominal, ordinal and interval/ratio.

Level of significance the level at which the researcher(s) will accept the results as not being due to chance but due to the manipulation in the study. In psychology, 0.05 or better (such as 0.01) is acceptable, 0.10 is not acceptable.

Long-term memory the third store for memory, according to the multi-store model. Information that is rehearsed passes from the short-term memory to the long-term memory.

Mann–Whitney U the statistical test used when difference is looked for, an independent groups design is used, and data are at least ordinal (they can be interval/ratio).

Memory encoding, storage and retrieval of experience. Without remembering, a person cannot function. There are different theories of memory, such as that it involves different levels of processing. Another theory suggests there is short-term and long-term memory.

Modality-specific when information is stored in the same form in which it is received. Information from the eyes is stored as an image, and from the ears is stored as sound.

Mode of representation the way memories are stored and the format they are stored in. A mode of representation or type of storage, could, for example, be visual or semantic.

Nominal a level of measurement that means data are in categories only, with no numbers assigned. If data include whether someone is aggressive or not, they are nominal data. Measures of central tendency are not useful here.

Non-directional hypothesis a hypothesis in which no direction is predicted and the results can be either 'more' or 'less'. For example, 'recall of letters is affected by whether or not letters are grouped (chunked)'.

Normal distribution when data are clustered in a 'bell shape' around the mean and the mean, median and mode are more or less the same, then data are normally distributed.

Null hypothesis the statement that any difference or relationship predicted in a study will be due to chance (in other words, there is no relationship or difference as predicted). It is the hypothesis that is tested when using statistical tests.

One-tailed when a hypothesis is directional (predicts the direction of the difference) then this is 'one-tailed' when checking critical values.

Operationalise to make a variable measurable. If you wanted to test helpfulness it would be difficult to know where to start, but you could operationalise helpfulness by measuring whether someone asking for directions was shown the way or not.

Order effects effects that occur when the order of conditions in a study (in a repeated measures design) affects the responses of the participant. They include fatigue and practice effects.

Ordinal a level of measurement that means data are ranked so that the smallest score has rank 1 and so on. The mode and median are suitable averages to use.

Outlier a score in a set of data that is very different from the rest is outlying and can affect the spread of scores, giving skewed distribution.

p < .05 the probability of the results being due to chance is equal to or less than 5%, which is 5 in 100 scores being due to chance (1 in 20).

Participant variables variables such as age, gender, experience and mood.

Phonological loop according to the working memory model, it deals with sound information. There is an articulatory loop where rehearsal takes place too. The phonological loop has been called the 'inner ear' and the articulatory loop has been called the 'inner voice'. This helps to explain what they are for.

Practice effect an order effect that occurs when the second part or condition of a study is done better than the first because participants are practised by the time they do the second condition.

Primary acoustic store in the working memory model part of the phonological loop, as well as the articulatory loop, is the primary acoustic store, for sound information other than speech.

Randomisation making the order in which the participant does the conditions random, to control for order effects in a repeated measures design. If a study has two conditions, for example, there can be a toss of the coin to see which condition the participant will do first.

Rationalisation shortening a story to make it make sense. This shows that memory is reconstructive, as Bartlett claimed.

Replicability the extent to which a study is easy to repeat or replicate. A study is replicable if there are careful controls and if there is enough detail about the procedure to do the study again.

Retrieval getting to the memories stored in the brain. A problem with retrieval will lead to forgetting. One theory suggests that retrieval can be aided by cues.

Schemata pre-existing ideas that have been built through experience and are plans for what we think will happen and what we know. For example, we might have a schema (the singular of schemata) for 'baking baked potatoes' or one for 'going on holiday on a train'. Our ideas affect how we remember events.

Semantic refers to the meaning of something. Semantic encoding would be registering the information in the form of its meaning, as you might with a word.

Semantic memory is memory that involves meaning, and episodic memory is part of this but specifically about episodes in our lives.

Sensory register the first store for memory, according to the multi-store model, where information comes into the brain from the senses. Information lasts less than a second and if it is attended to it goes to the short-term store. If it is not attended to it is then not available. Information is stored in the same form as it is received, so is modality-specific. Information from the eyes is stored as an image, and from the ears is stored as sound.

Short-term memory the second store for memory, according to the multi-store model. Information that is attended to in the sensory register passes to the short-term memory; if it is then rehearsed it gets to the long-term memory.

Situational variables variables to do with the situation, such as temperature, noise, interruptions and light.

Skewed distribution when there is one or more outlying score and the mean, median and mode of a data set are not the same, data are skewed. This affects statistical testing and drawing conclusions.

Spearman's the statistical test when a correlation is being used and data are at least ordinal (they can be interval/ratio).

Standardised instructions written sets of instructions to the participants in a study so that all participants get the same information and are not biased by being told something different.

Storage the retention of information ready for retrieval. One type of forgetting is a problem with storage, another type can be a problem with retrieval.

Theory an idea about why an event happens, usually based on previous theories and research.

Glossary

Two-tailed when a hypothesis is non-directional (does not predict the direction of the difference) then this is 'two-tailed' when checking critical values.

Variables whatever influences are likely to affect the experiment, including what is being tested, what is being measured, and anything else likely to affect the results. They include confounding variables, extraneous variables, the independent variable and the dependent variable. There are also situational variables and participant variables.

Visuospatial sketchpad according to the working memory model, it deals with visual information. The scratchpad/sketchpad holds spatial information and information about images. The scratchpad could be called the 'inner eye'.

Wilcoxon signed rank test the statistical test used when difference is looked for, a repeated measures or matched pairs design is used, and data are at least ordinal (they can be interval/ratio).

Knowledge check answers

1 Social psychology involves the study of interactions between people and of group behaviour. It concerns how people live together and the processes, such as obedience to those in authority or issues around prejudice and discrimination (e.g. looking at football fan violence).

2 Experiment 7 found that 9 out of 40 obeyed to the maximum voltage (22.5%) and it was concluded that there was much less obedience to phone orders. If the experimenter was not present in the room, the participant obeyed less. Experiment 10 found 19 obeyed out of 40 (47.5%). It was concluded that in a rundown office block there was lower obedience, however, other features of authority were present such as the generator and the experimenter, so perhaps the setting itself was not the only feature giving obedience in the main study. Experiment 13 found that just 4 of the 20 participants in this variation obeyed to the maximum voltage (20%) and it was concluded that the appearance of the experimenter did have some effect on obedience.

3 a) A strength is the evidence from variations — the less they were agents, the less participants obeyed. b) A weakness is that there are other explanations, such as social power theory — Milgram had expert power and legitimate power. c) A strength is the power of the explanation in real-life situations. The idea can be used to account for acts carried out by people (e.g. in the Holocaust) that are so hard to understand. d) A weakness is the lack of depth in the explanation: obedience is being the agent of an authority figure, because of being their agent — this is tautological.

4 Milgram found when other 'teachers' were present and did not obey, obedience dropped (to 10%) — showing that the presence of others had an impact on the participant's decision making. Milgram found that when the experimenter was replaced by an 'ordinary man', obedience dropped a lot too (to 20%) — showing an expert, seen as 'strong' in the sense of message-giving, seemed to get more obedience. When there was more than one experimenter, and one told the participant to stop, all participants stopped. The original study, where 65% obeyed to the maximum voltage, showed that being told what to do by someone in authority was enough. All these findings suggest that others have an impact on what we do.

5 A football team is likely to see themselves as an in-group and an opposing side as the out-group, which is social identification. They will categorise themselves as an in-group, including wearing team colours, which is social categorisation. Then they will compare their team with an opposing team, seeing the other team as 'bad' and themselves as 'better', which is social comparison. Seeing themselves as better and feeling hostility (prejudice) to the out-group enhances the self-esteem of members, which helps to keep them together as an in-group.

6 Realistic conflict theory explains that it is not just being in two (or more) groups that brings prejudice and discrimination, but that there must also be conflict or competition between the two groups. Lalonde (1992) showed how a hockey team boosted their self-esteem by denigrating the out-group (another team), however, the two teams were also in competition. Perhaps it is the conflict (e.g. over resources) that leads to the prejudice so SIT is not enough on its own to explain prejudice. Another weakness is that prejudice is complex, some groups coexist in harmony, such as different nationalities in Switzerland, and SIT does not capture such complexity.

7 Becker et al. (2012) looked at data from 21 cultural groups. They included information about personality and found that there were cultural effects on prejudice that were more than personal beliefs and attitudes. Guimond et al. (2013) found similar evidence for there being cultural factors in prejudice. They found that the more multicultural the norms of a country and the more the country's policy reflected those norms, the less prejudice was found. They found Canada was the least prejudiced and Germany the most, with the USA and UK in between. Germany was the least multicultural.

8 The aim is to see if there are gender differences in in-group favouritism. The IV is whether the participant is male or female. The DV is how many points are given.

9 Qualitative data give richer detail than quantitative data. This means that data are more valid, in that the respondent has the opportunity to interpret a question or statement in their own way rather than being constrained into answering in the way a researcher suggests. Quantitative data are not as rich because they often involve ticking 'yes' or 'no' or rating statements. No matter how much better quantitative data are to analyse (such as yielding percentages for comparisons), qualitative data have more value in that they are about real-life situations and attitudes.

10 Questionnaires ask people for their own opinions and feelings — these are self-report data. People can say they would do something, such as help someone, or say they would not do something, such as give what they think is an electric shock to someone. However, it cannot be known whether they would actually do what they say they would do. In many ways, none of us can know what we would do in a certain situation until it arose. Therefore, questionnaires do not measure actual behaviour. Attitudes may not reflect behaviour.

11 Example: informed consent and right to withdraw. Informed consent means that the participant must know what the study is about and what they have to do before they agree to take part, and they must give informed agreement before the start of the study. Even though they have given informed consent and been deceived as little as possible, throughout the study they must be given the right to withdraw

and the offer must be repeated explicitly and often. They must feel able to withdraw, and this includes withdrawing their data after the study has ended.

12 There are structured, unstructured and semi-structured interviews. Structured interviews are good because answers from one respondent can be compared with those from another as they are asked the same things — this is likely to lead to reliability. Unstructured interviews are good because the interviewer can go with the respondent's answers and follow threads that would not be available in a structured interview, which means data are more rich and valid. Semi-structured interviews are good because topics are focused on and so there is structure for comparison of results and yet data can be valid because of open questioning.

13 The standard deviation shows how far scores vary from the mean and is a measure of dispersion, like the range but it gives more detail.

14 'Being liked' is one theme, 'how others are seen' is another theme, and 'liking new people' can be a theme. 'Not seeing self as prejudiced' might be a theme and 'people are not nice' might also be a theme.

15 Descriptive statistics summarise numbers. The mode, median and mean, as well as graphs and charts, all require numbers. Qualitative data are in the form of words and need a different type of analysis. For example, someone's attitudes to people in different groups could range from interested and supportive to hostile and aggressive, and none of these comments could be summarised using numbers. Qualitative data can be grouped into categories and then would become quantitative data if numbers in categories became the data, but in their raw form qualitative data are not suitable for statistical analysis.

16 In a study in psychology there can be risk to participants, the researcher(s), bystanders, the environment, or to society. Socially sensitive research can affect members of society as can research that is used for social control. People should not be harmed in a study, according to BPS ethical guidelines. The BPS guidelines discuss management of risk too, emphasising its need, in particular for vulnerable people, when keeping records, because of labelling, when there might be harm and if biological samples are to be used. Researchers must adhere to BPS guidelines if they are BPS members, for the sake of their own career as well, of course, to protect others.

17 The Robber's Cave study found that even without meeting, the two groups of boys became hostile once they knew about each other, supporting the social identity claim about in-group favouritism and out-group hostility. Then when there was competition between the boys, such as for a cup, which is a limited resource, hostility increased, such as one burning the other's flag. This supports the realistic conflict theory.

18 Burger, like Milgram, used laboratory experiments with carefully set up procedures that could be replicated for each participant, meaning data could be compared. Sherif et al. used a field experiment, which also had carefully set up procedures, such as how sampling was done, including matching. However, Sherif et al. did their experiment in a setting natural for the participants, a summer camp, whereas Burger's lab situation was not natural for the participants. This naturalness in the setting and situation is what distinguishes a field experiment from a lab experiment. Also in Sherif's field study, though there were experiments, data were gathered by other means as well, such as observation, which was not the case in Burger's study.

19 US soldiers in Iraq were controlling Iraqi prisoners of war in the Abu Ghraib prison. In 2004, it was reported in newspapers that the soldiers had been acting brutally towards the prisoners and pictures showed the horrific nature of the soldiers' acts. The soldiers were assumed not to be evil as individuals. It was wondered why what appeared to be 'normal' people had done (or were doing) such terrible acts against other human beings. Members of the public wanted answers and there were calls for punishment for such acts.

20 Example: I used opportunity sampling because I used the sixth-form students who were in the common room at the time I wanted to do my study and I gave all of them my questionnaire to complete. I gave them the right to withdraw by writing on the top of each questionnaire that they did not have to complete it, could miss questions out and could leave the study at any time.

21 Cognitive psychology looks at how the brain processes information, by looking at models of what might happen and at actual brain structures and functioning (neuroscience). One example is the multi-store model which shows how information is input via the senses, processed through various stores, including getting information into long-term memory, and then there is output. This model clearly shows that cognitive psychology involves information processing. The idea of the brain being like a computer is another example, which the multi-store model also encompasses, with its focus on input-throughput-output.

22 Both the multi-store and working memory models look at processing of information between it coming into the brain and it going into long-term memory. However, a difference is working memory applies to all processing and not just memory, for example, it involves perception. The working memory model involves a central executive, which is a control centre, whereas the multi-store model does not look at control over processing. The two are similar, however, in having limited capacity processing (short-term) between information coming in and it being retained for longer.

23 Experiments are strongly controlled so that it can be claimed that the IV causes the change in DV, whereas other methods might not be able to claim a cause-and-effect difference so clearly. Experiments have standardised procedures so they are replicable. If studies can be redone and the same results found, the findings are reliable. Other methods tend not to be so standardised so not so easy to repeat. Experiments can take a specific part of the theory, operationalise the variables and then test that specific part, whereas other methods may not be able to operationalise as clearly, and therefore not have such credible findings.

24 Noise can be a situational variable. Noise in the setting of a study can distract participants or can be greater for one condition than the other so can affect results. Hunger is a participant variable. One group may do the study just after lunch and the other just before lunch. Such differences can affect performance.

25 **Differences**: a) A field experiment is done in surroundings that are natural for the participants, whereas a laboratory experiment is done in an artificial setting. b) In a field experiment, it is hard to control for extraneous variables because the natural setting implies variables that are not controllable, such as traffic noise or temperature. However, in a laboratory setting, variables are a lot more controllable. **Similarities**: a) In both a field and a laboratory experiment, there is an IV involving conditions that are manipulated by the researcher. b) In both a field and a laboratory experiment, planning is such that cause-and-effect conclusions are aimed for, so controls are as tight as they can be so that the IV manipulation can be said to *cause* the DV.

26 A directional hypothesis might be 'boys are more aggressive/rougher in the playground as scored by the number of aggressive and rough acts than girls'.

27 a) Independent groups could be useful as the participant does not have to do more than one condition so will not learn and get better, for example (or get bored). This would be good for two lists of words, with a different condition each, as then the words could be the same. b) Repeated measures could be useful as it takes away participant differences, so it would work well when learning words underwater and on land. c) A matched pairs design can be good when the conditions need different people (such as when needing to use the same word list) and can also take away participant differences. In a study where one condition was learning in a quiet room and one was learning in a noisy room, the same materials could be used.

28 Two ways of avoiding order effects include counterbalancing (the order of presentation of conditions is alternated) and randomising the order of conditions (e.g. a coin is tossed each time). A third way, if practicable, is to use an independent groups design: there will not be order effects as different people do each condition so will not get tired (fatigue effect) or get better at the task (practice effect).

29 The test is the Wilcoxon signed rank test.

30 Nominal data.

31 There is no significant difference between words remembered from a list of 30 depending on whether someone is 60 years old or over compared with someone aged 20 to 30 years. Any difference there is will be due to chance or some other factor.

32 The Mann–Whitney U-test is for an independent groups design so there are different participants in each group and there might be different numbers in the groups. For example, there might be a group of 15 people aged 60 and over compared with a group of 12 people aged 20 to 30 years. N_1 would be 15 and N_2 would be 12. The Wilcoxon test is for a repeated measures or matched pairs design so the same participants (or 'as if' the same) would do the different conditions, just one number for N (N=number of participants).

33 Baddeley (1966b) used two different conditions and two control conditions to match. He used two lists focusing on auditory similarity, so one list had 10 words that sounded alike and there was another list that matched (in length and so on) but the words did not sound alike. He used two lists focusing on semantic similarity, so one list had 10 words with similar meaning and there was another list that matched but the words did not have similar meaning.

34 (1) They wanted to find out how digit span changed from 5 year olds to 17 year olds, to see the developmental pattern to adulthood.
(2) They wanted to see if the developmental pattern matched what was found in studies of English speakers.
(3) They wanted to look at healthy older people compared with those with Alzheimer's and those with another form of dementia and to compare their digit spans with one another as well as with 5 to 17 year olds.

35 Making up acronyms would help rehearsal by shortening the 'chunks' to remember (e.g. GRAVE for evaluating studies — generalisability, reliability, application, validity, ethics — but making up your own). Imagining the revision session when in the exam, or having actual cues (again perhaps an acronym as a mnemonic), might help to give schemas to help to reconstruct the memories accurately.

36 Example: The IV was whether the participant used rehearsal in the study or did the interference task that blocked rehearsal. The DV was the number of letters recalled from the list given. One control was that the letters were the same for both conditions, in the same order and presented in the same timing. The right to withdraw was given at the start, halfway through (with a reminder) and at the end (at the debrief, to ask if they were happy for their data to be used).

Index

Index